Literacy-Building Play in Preschool

Lit Kits, Prop Boxes, and Other Easy-to-Make Tools to Boost Emergent Reading and Writing Skills Through Dramatic Play

V. Susan Bennett-Armistead

📖 SCHOLASTIC

New York • Toronto • London • Auckland • Sydney
Mexico City • New Delhi • Hong Kong • Buenos Aires

For Dave, who's been there from the beginning,
and understands.

Editor: Raymond Coutu

Interior Designer: Maria Lilja

Cover Designer: Jorge Namerow

Cover Photos: Maria Lilja and Raymond Coutu

Interior Photos: Maria Lilja and Raymond Coutu, unless otherwise noted

Copy Editor: Eileen Judge

ISBN-10: 0-545-08748-1

ISBN-13: 978-0-545-08748-3

1 2 3 4 5 6 7 8 9 10   46   16 15 14 13 12 11 10 09

Contents

Acknowledgments

This is my first book I've written without coauthors. I'd like to think it's the first book I've written by myself. But, of course, no one really writes a book by herself. Every book has many contributors.

I have had the privilege of visiting the Associated Services for Children and Youth in Hamilton, Ontario, several times over the last couple of years. It was there that I first saw their marvelous collection of dramatic play theme trunks. Evette Sauriol generously talked me through how she and the other early literacy specialists, Brenda Jenner, Maria Agro, and Kim Burns, create and use them, and she helped me photograph them for this book. Evette's enthusiasm and her trunks were the spark for this book. It would not be in your hands were it not for her.

The teachers and children depicted in this book are from real classrooms. Thanks to all the parents for permitting their children's images to be included and congratulations for selecting such wonderful programs for those children. Thank you to Mary Pat Vollick, executive director, and Brianne St. Louis, Lina Seeley, Ethel Corbin, and Lisa Vaudry, teachers, at the Pumpkin Patch Mount Hamilton Baptist Day Care Centre in Hamilton, Ontario, who shared their wonderful ideas for using theme trunks in their literacy-rich classrooms. A special thank you to my colleagues and students at the Katherine Durst Child Development Laboratories at the University of Maine, including Margo Brown, Callie Scronce, and Kim Smith. They bravely allowed me to come in, observe, and photograph them, and raid their collections of children's work for examples to use in this book. Thank you all for helping other teachers to see the amazing things you offer.

My sister, Sheila Bennett, helped "clean up" the booklists in the appendix. She is a speedy, efficient editor who has saved me many times over the years.

Most important, I am deeply indebted to my editor, Ray Coutu. This is our fourth book together. With each one, I marvel at his patience, his surgical skill in cutting to the point I'm trying to make (even when I don't do it well), and his understanding of what readers want. For this book, he also stretched his creative muscle and shot many of the photos. I'm honored to know him and hope we can enjoy many more collaborations.

Finally, I am thankful to all the teachers over the years who have so generously shared their practice, their thinking about dramatic play, and their efforts to maximize its benefits for children. You inspired the direction of this book and will, surely, influence many other teachers in years to come. Thank you all!

—V. Susan Bennett-Armistead

Chapter 1

Raising the Curtain on Dramatic Play

"Vroom! Vroom! Here comes the police car. We'll help you, ma'am!"

"I have an important letter for you. You better read it."

"Their house is on fire! Check the map. We have to get there fast!"

What Is Dramatic Play?

Play is many things to many people. For most of us, it is a self-selected, self-directed activity that children carry out for pleasure. In fact, many leaders in our field, such as David Elkind, Vivian Paley, and Lilian Katz have referred to play as "children's work" because it provides rich opportunities to learn concepts such as cause and effect ("If you hit a tower of blocks, it will fall down.") and time relationships ("I will play dress-up with you after lunch, at choice time."). It also helps children gain understandings of how the world works ("Some things float and some things sink."), how to get along with others ("If you take Billy's truck, he will scream at you."), how to entertain one's self ("Fingerpaint feels awesome between your toes!"), and how to solve problems ("Fingerpaint is really hard to get off your toes.").

But don't let that definition let you forget an essential point: play should be fun. The Association for Child Development defines play in its position statement as a "dynamic, active and constructive behavior" that is "essential for all children" (ACEI, 2002). Fun matters. It's what gets children engaged, curious, and coming back for more.

In this book, I focus on a specific kind of play: dramatic play or, as it's sometimes called, pretend play, imitative play, and symbolic play, which usually involves:

- reenacting everyday activities or situations that children observe, such as diapering a baby

- engaging in intensely imaginative activities based on knowledge children gain from books, movies, and other sources, such as exploring the tropical jungle

- retelling and/or reenacting stories they hear, such as *The Three Little Pigs*

- singing and acting out songs they hear, such as "Twinkle, Twinkle Little Star" and "The Itsy Bitsy Spider".

This book shows you ways to use engaging, rich dramatic play experiences to meet your curricular goals and build your children's developing literacy skills.

These children are reenacting a favorite story, *The Three Little Pigs,* and learning important lessons about literacy in the process.

What Is the Value of Dramatic Play?

I confess. The dramatic-play area is my favorite area in a classroom. There are few other places where children can be as creative and explore so many new ideas. They can spend time as paleontologists hunting for fossils one week and as deep-sea explorers the next. The abandon children exhibit while engaged in dramatic play is enthralling.

Of course, dramatic play shouldn't happen only in a designated area. The block area may contain an elaborate highway system, for example, with children engaged in different roles such as architects designing buildings, delivery people dropping off materials, police officers patrolling traffic, and construction workers maintaining the highway.

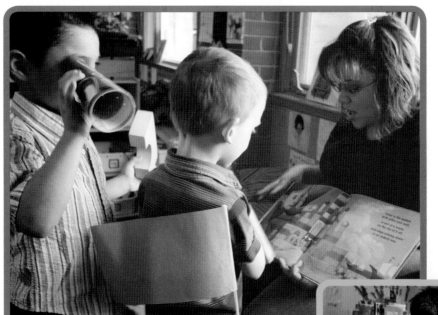

This block play was inspired by a teacher's read aloud. The children created a boat and then used it to pretend to sail away. When uncertain about the boat's design features, they checked back with the text for ideas.

The playground's sandbox might be a great place for a sandcastle—the base for medieval knights about to set out on a crusade. The climber might be the tower where Rapunzel is being held captive by the Wicked Witch. Children might compose letters in the writing center to mail in the dramatic-play area's post office. Dramatic play is important no matter where it occurs. I could watch for hours.

Beyond being fun, dramatic play serves young children in other important ways. It allows them to experiment with roles that are familiar to them, experiment with roles that are unfamiliar to them, work through issues that are troubling them, and explore concepts to make them their own. In this section, I discuss how dramatic play can help children engage in these literacy-building experiences.

Children experiment with roles that are familiar to them.

Toddlers and young preschoolers enjoy playing "house," assuming the roles of mother, father, sister, and brother, because they know that world so intimately. They typically enjoy playing waiter or cook at a restaurant or teacher at a preschool for a similar reason: they have spent significant time in those places. By assuming these roles, children increase their understandings of how things work (You put the dirty clothes and soap in the washer and then you move the clothes to the dryer.), how "players" function independently and relate to one another (A waiter takes your order and then passes it onto the cook.), and the specialized vocabulary used in the environment (soiled, detergent, cycle, shift, value, appetizer, hostess, receipt, and so forth).

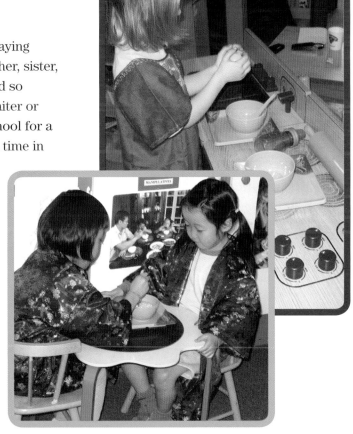

The housekeeping area offers children the opportunity to play out familiar experiences such as preparing and enjoying a meal. Including clothing and pretend food that honor the children's ethnic diversity ensures that each child can make a connection.

These little girls are playing with ponies as if they are a mommy and baby living in a doll's house. These roles are familiar to them, even if the family life of ponies is not.

Children might also retell favorite stories using puppets or flannel boards, which helps them gain important comprehension skills such as understanding story sequence, important vocabulary, character motivation, and key events in the plot.

Children experiment with roles that are unfamiliar to them.

Once children are comfortable assuming familiar roles, they typically assume less familiar ones, such as a doctor or a cashier. You can enhance their play by taking them on a fieldtrip to a hospital or grocery store where children can see real people in those roles. As children's world experience and imagination skills grow, their play becomes more complex and abstract. You may observe them pretending to fly a space shuttle, which is something they've never done, but can envision doing by drawing on what they know about transportation and space exploration. This kind of creativity results not only in rich play, but in rich storytelling, which is an essential skill for writing that children will do later in their school careers.

Children work through issues that are troubling them.

Older preschoolers can take on the roles of fictional characters and act out situations they find frightening or that make them feel out of control (Kostelnik, Whiren & Stein, 1986). For example, pretending to be a superhero who protects a classmate from a bully might empower a child who is being bullied himself. It may give the child a sense of mastery over someone or something he or she fears.

Superhero play is ideal for the dramatic play area because it invites children to act out situations using a variety of materials, including print-rich materials. For example, this superhero is using a stop sign to warn of danger in the block area.

Children explore concepts to make them their own.

Most people learn best through *primary experiences*, that is, experiences they've had rather than experiences they've heard about. Dramatic play allows for near-primary experiences. It can make the abstract real for children. Most children will never get to go in a submarine or to the rainforest. However, through dramatic play, they can gain understandings nearly as rich as if they were having the experience. For example, after listening to Robert McCloskey's *Make Way for Ducklings*, a group of children wanted to reenact the story. At one point in their play, one little Mama Duck stood up and announced, "Someone get me some food. I can't because I'm molting!" She had understood that the term *molting* meant that the mother duck would have had difficulty leaving her nest owing to a loss of feathers. While this child will never experience molting herself, she has gained a strong understanding of the term because she created a very authentic experience—in her mind, a primary experience—related to it. Sometimes primary experiences are not possible or even desirable. (Think "shark attack!") Dramatic play is the next best thing.

For children to truly make concepts their own, teachers need to take an active role in guiding their play. There are suggestions throughout this book on how to do that.

Key Terms

Throughout this book, I use terms that may be unfamiliar to you to describe areas and activities that can enrich dramatic play, such as

Literacy Center: A literacy center is a designated part of the room for play-time activities designed to build children's reading, writing, speaking, and listening skills, such as alphabet matching activities and rhyming games.

Dress-Up Area: One of several activity areas in a classroom, the dress-up area is a designated area with costumes and accessories designed to encourage children's pretend play.

Choice Time: Choice time is a predetermined point in the day when children move freely about the room, selecting from a variety of activities you set up, such as painting and block play.

Lit Kit: Short for "literacy kit," a lit kit is a collection of props and/or activities inspired by a favorite children's book, such as *The Very Hungry Caterpillar* or *The Snowy Day*, often stored in a shoebox-sized plastic bin. (See Chapter 2 for more information.)

Flannel Board: A flannel board is a fabric-covered board that children use as a surface for telling or retelling stories, using cut-outs of significant characters and objects from those stories. (See Chapter 3 for more information.)

Prop Box: Also known as dramatic play kits or prop kits, a prop box is a collection of objects for use in a theme-based activity center, such as a restaurant, farm, or hospital. (See Chapter 4 for more information.)

Theme Trunk: A super-sized prop box of sorts, a theme trunk contains not only props inspired by a particular theme, but also costumes and a collection of theme-related books. (See Chapter 5 for more information.)

How Does Dramatic Play Support Literacy Development?

Dramatic play has many general benefits as discussed above. But, more specifically, it can build skills in powerful ways by allowing children to experiment with purposes for literacy they've seen at home, to recognize that different tasks require different texts, to produce a wide variety of texts, and to act out stories they have heard. In this section, I discuss each of these benefits.

Dramatic play allows children to experiment with purposes for literacy they've seen at home.

By including functional print, such as newspapers, personal letters, menus, shelf signs, coupons, and labeled food containers, in children's play and giving them paper and pens for writing, we create an environment that allows them to interact with print as adults do. We give them a chance to see, first hand, the many ways we use text in everyday life. This is very different from what happens during group time, when we tend to read books. Researchers Susan Neuman and Kathleen Roskos (1993) found that classrooms rich in functional print inspired more literacy-focused dramatic play, which resulted in children with greater literacy competencies.

Dramatic play allows children to recognize that different tasks require different texts.

By regularly and systematically incorporating literacy props into dramatic play, you help children realize that different tasks require different texts. For example, the firefighters might need a map of the city to locate emergencies, but the veterinarian needs an appointment book and pamphlets about pet care to hand out to her patients' owners. The restaurant has menus and order pads, but the flower shop has seed packets and price lists. This exposure to a wide range of texts helps children differentiate text features—even very young children. For example, children tend to format a shopping list differently from the way they format a map. (See examples on the next page.)

Chapter 4, on prop boxes, offers suggestions for including a variety of functional texts in dramatic play, from discount coupons to flight manuals.

This map was created by a child who wanted to give "Good Guys" directions to find to "Bad Guys," which he represents with orange dots. The red triangle tells readers "you are here." For more on "Good Guy/Bad Guy" play, see page 82.

This shopping list was created by a child who wanted to capture all the items needed for his upcoming birthday party. While it's not clear precisely what he needs because his letter strings don't align with the sounds of words, it's safe to assume the word starting with "k" is "cake."

Dramatic play allows children to produce a wide variety of texts.

Many of us are drawn to storybooks because that's what we were raised on. However, there are so many more options for young children today. By exposing children to a wide variety of functional texts, we encourage them to create a wide variety of functional text, too. Children might make traffic signs to post in the block area, a list for use at the grocery store, a receipt for a customer at the pizza shop, or a letter to a friend to mail at the post office. When children see multiple purposes for text, they are more likely to find a purpose that matters to them. In short, by exposing children to many texts and giving them the opportunity to create their own, they are more likely to include text in their lives, not just in their play.

Although this child is still at the scribble stage of writing, it doesn't stop him from composing a message to a friend to mail at the dramatic play post office.

Dramatic play builds comprehension by allowing children to act out familiar stories.

Acting out and/or retelling a story helps children make that story their own—and truly comprehend it. They gain an understanding of the characters, the structure, and the themes. For example, after reading Paul Galdone's version of the *Three Billy Goats Gruff*, try encouraging children to act out the story. By taking on different roles, they will gain an understanding that characters have different personalities and motivations. They will learn that the story unfolds in a certain way: the littlest billy goat goes over the bridge first, then the midsized goat, then the biggest goat, and so on.

In the process, young children gain a sophisticated understanding of narrative structure. Chapter 2, on literacy kits, offers easy-to-set-up activities for favorite stories. In Chapter 3, on flannel boards and puppet play, I share suggestions for promoting retellings. Chapters 4 and 5, on prop boxes and theme trunks respectively, show you how to maximize opportunities to act out stories and other texts children have heard. The result? Children wind up with the baseline skills they need to read and write.

These children are preparing for dramatic play by taking a closer look at the story their teacher read to them, *Little Red Riding Hood*.

How to Use This Book

There is no one right way to use this book, but here are some ideas to consider:

🌀 Read it from beginning to end, adopting what is most valuable to you.

🌀 Select a literacy tool that intrigues you, such as lit kits, read the appropriate chapter, and start gathering materials.

🌀 Try something you've never tried before—a prop box, for example. Select a theme and create one—just one—to see how it works. I suspect you'll want to create more from there. (You'll find many suggestions for themes in Chapter 4.)

🌀 Get together with other teachers to create a collection of prop boxes or theme trunks that you all can use. Each of you can take responsibility for one or two boxes or trunks, gathering the books and/or materials suggested in Chapters 4 and 5.

🌀 Use the big ideas scattered throughout the book to help you talk with colleagues, parents, and administrators about the value of dramatic play. Chapter 7 may be particularly helpful because it offers answers to questions that you may be asking yourself or that others may ask you.

🌀 Use the appendix to create libraries. It offers book suggestions organized around 25 tried-and-true themes.

Dramatic play will enrich your program and the lives of the children in your care. The best part is you'll have fun doing it!

Concluding Thoughts

In this book, I focus on promoting emergent reading and writing skills through dramatic play. It is possible, of course, to incorporate math, science, social studies, and other curriculum areas into play as well. The key is planning purposefully. As you read, think about your goals for children. In what way can you make a concept "real" to them? What kinds of play experiences might bring the concept alive and allow for children to make connections to things they already know? For example, if your goal is to help children understand that stories have characters, here's what you might do:

- Select a text that has characters, such as *Goldilocks and the Three Bears*.

- Read the story to the children, perhaps a couple of times so that they become very familiar with it.

- Consider reenacting the story, using flannel cut-outs of each character— or have the children *be* the characters. Or do both: tell the story using the flannel board pieces, make the flannel board pieces available for the children so they can tell the story, and then act the story out in small groups.

- Place appropriate costumes and props in the dress-up area so the children can act out the story on their own time.

Contrast this approach with simply telling the children, "The characters in *Goldilocks and the Three Bears* are Goldilocks, Papa Bear, Mama Bear, and Baby Bear." Using dramatic play helps children understand the concept of "character," the relationships between the characters, and the concept of story so much more effectively. In many ways, it's the difference between seeing a picture of chocolate and actually tasting it. You understand it differently for having experienced it.

Through play, you can meet all your curricular goals—and enjoy yourself in the process. In the following chapters, I discuss specific tools—literacy kits, puppets, flannel boards, prop boxes, and theme trunks—to help you do just that.

Chapter 2

Literacy Kits

Whether we call it the book nook, literacy area, reading corner, or the library, most of us have a space in the classroom filled with children's books and supporting materials, such as a CD or tape player with recorded stories, a computer, flannel boards, and puppets. But only a few classrooms I've visited also include literacy kits or, as they're more commonly known, "lit kits"—a wonderful addition to any learning environment. This chapter shows you how to create and use lit kits.

What Is a Lit Kit?

Think of a lit kit as a literacy center in a box. A typical kit contains a picture book and the props necessary for carrying out an activity designed to promote children's understanding of that book. More elaborate kits might have a couple of versions of the same story, for example Jan Brett's and Alvin Tresselt's versions of *The Mitten*, and props for several activities. Often these kits include a game inspired by the story and masks or small toys for acting out the story. A lit kit for *The Mitten*, for instance, might contain a large felt mitten and plastic animals to represent each character.

Typical components of a lit kit

What Does a Lit Kit Contain?

Lit kits are usually used by children independently or with one or two friends. Therefore, a high priority should be placed on selecting texts that children are familiar with and props they can easily figure out. Plan to support the play initially, in case children need assistance in figuring out how to use the materials.

The book and props can be stored in everyday sturdy containers, such as plastic stacking bins or pizza boxes. Each kit should be labeled with the title of the book and contain a list of its contents, which allows you to quickly make sure all materials are present and to replace anything that's missing. (For more information on storage, see page 27.)

A typical storage system for lit kits

How to Use a Lit Kit

The kits can be used in a variety of ways. You can use them for teaching small groups or the whole class. You can set them out for children's independent use during choice time or send them home by putting the contents in a bag and attaching a letter like the one below. However you use the kits, make sure the children are familiar with the book and the materials first so children know the story well enough to act it out with the props.

Sending lit kits home is a great way to get parents involved and extend learning.

Dear Family Member:

Your child has brought home a literacy kit! As you explore it together, you will find a book, some toys that go with it, and some things to talk about while you read and play. I hope the time you spend together reading and responding to this book is memorable—for both of you! You may want to write down what your child says or have your child create a picture about the book.

Keep in mind, this activity is more than just fun. It is critical to your child's literacy development. Being read to, talking about books, acting out stories, and thinking about related stories in other books and in life will help your child gain skills needed for later reading and writing success. There are so many ways to interact with books. We hope you enjoy discovering many this week. Please return the kit to school on Monday.

Sincerely,

Your child's teacher

For small-group and whole-class instruction, start by reading the book aloud. If the book is a story, consider reading it multiple times so children become familiar enough with it to retell important details and talk about the structure, themes, and characters. If the book is an informational text, read various sections aloud and talk about what you learn from them and what you'd still like to learn. After you've read and discussed the book, introduce the accompanying activity, such as finger puppets that invite students to retell the story or a game that requires them to remember key events. (The list on pages 23–27 gives you some ideas for activities.) While activities such as these would not be appropriate for the whole class to do at once, you can encourage children to select the activity during choice time by demonstrating how to carry it out. It might also be possible to modify a game to include all children. For example, a story may only have three goats and a troll, but who says there can't be six little goats, four medium goats, five big goats, and three trolls? A little flexibility and a lot of creativity can go a long way.

Lit kits inspired by Bill Martin, Jr.'s *Brown Bear, Brown Bear, What Do You See?* and Jim Arnosky's *Rabbits & Raindrops*.

Book Title	Props	Suggested Activities
The Best Bug Parade by Stuart Murphy	a wide array of plastic bugs, two of each type	Have the children find matching pairs of bugs. Talk about what is the same and what is different. How did the children know what made a "pair?" Line the pairs up for a parade. Further activities might identify the actual types of insects. This is also well suited to *Insect* by Penelope Arlon listed on the next page.
Blueberries for Sal by Robert McCloskey	a girl doll, a mom doll, a large stuffed bear, a baby bear, a small metal bucket	Have the children retell the story using the props.
Chicka Chicka Boom Boom by Bill Martin, Jr., and John Archambault	a felt coconut tree, all the upper and lower case letters cut from felt	Have the children retell the story. Match lower case letters to upper case letters. What words can they make from the letters?
Color Dance by Ann Jonas	scarves of different colors	Encourage the children to dance with the scarves. Have them guess what colors will result when two colors are mixed together. Keep a chart of their predictions.
The Doorbell Rang by Pat Hutchins	12 felt or cardboard cookies, 12 plates, one plate with additional cookies	Have the children divide the cookies as you read the story. Before you read a page, ask them how many cookies each child will get.

Book Title	Props	Suggested Activities
Fancy Nancy by Jane O'Connor	sequins, mask forms, feathers, glue sticks, beads	Have the children decorate a mask to make it fancy.
Growing Vegetable Soup by Lois Ehlert	seed packets for vegetables, soil, small containers for growing plants, plant journal	Have the children select which vegetables they'd like to grow. Plant a seed. Have children chronicle the changes over time. How tall is their plant in the first week? The second? Does their plant get flowers on it? Keep a plant journal or poster to document the changes.
Good Night, Gorilla by Peggy Rathmann	plastic animals of each character in the story, as well as a doll for the zookeeper	Have the children act out the story, saying goodnight to each animal.
In the Small, Small Pond by Denise Fleming	plastic creatures depicted in the book	Place the creatures in the water table and have the children retell the story.
Insect by Penelope Arlon (Eye Know series)	bug jar, plastic insects, bug or fishing nets	Hide plastic insects around the room. Have the children locate and identify the insects by looking them up in the book.

Book Title	Props	Suggested Activities
The Jolly Postman or *The Jolly Christmas Postman* by Allan and Janet Ahlberg	stationery and envelopes	Have the children write or dictate a letter to their favorite fairytale characters.
The Mitten by Jan Brett	a large felt mitten and plastic animals for each character in the story	Have the children retell the story by placing each animal into the mitten as they tell it. Have them scatter when the bear sneezes!
Mouse Paint by Ellen Stoll Walsh	color paddles, color lenses, or actual paint	Encourage the children to overlay the color paddles or lenses. If using paint, have them mix the paint into new colors. Have them guess what colors will result when two colors are mixed together. Keep a chart of their predictions.
On the Road by Susan Steggall	a toy car, the phrases "along the road," "past the garage," "up the hill," "around the corner," etc., written on cards	Place the words in a sequence and have the children take turns driving the car in the order of the phrases on the cards. Mix up the cards and repeat.

Book Title	Props	Suggested Activities
A Pair of Socks by Stuart Murphy	actual or felt socks in a wide range of jazzy colors and designs (about 10 pairs)	Mix up the socks and have the children match the pairs. Talk about *same* and *different*.
Owl Babies by Martin Waddell	a nest, three small plastic or stuffed owls, one large owl	Have the children act out the story, using the repeated phrase "I want my mama!" What would they do if they missed their mama?
Stellaluna by Janel Cannon	bird finger puppets, cloth nest, bat finger puppet, plastic bugs and fruit	Have the children wear the finger puppets while retelling the story using the props.
Surprising Sharks by Nicola Davies	plastic sharks of various types, poster showing a variety of shark types, fishnets	Have the children play with the sharks in the water table. They scoop up the specimen with a net and identify the type using Davies's book and/or a poster. This activity can be adapted for books on rocks, frogs, fossils, insects, etc. Consider varying how the children locate the materials: sand table, outside sandbox, trunk filled with packing peanuts, etc.
Sylvester and the Magic Pebble by William Steig	a small red glass pebbles (available in craft or discount stores for use in the bottoms of vases), three plastic donkeys (Sylvester and his parents), a rock the size of the donkey, a plastic lion	Have the children retell the story using the props. Follow up by giving the children their own magic pebbles. Have them write or tell what they would wish for if they could wish for anything.

Book Title	Props	Suggested Activities
Zootles **Animal Babies issue** This magazine, published by Zoobooks, focuses on a different theme each month. A kit can be made for each issue.	Animal Baby Lotto or Memory games	Have the children play the games and compare the names of babies to the names of their parents, such as foal–horse, cub–lion, chick–chicken, etc.

Lit Kit Storage

Sturdy plastic stacking bins are handy containers for lit kits. Again, each kit should contain one book, along with its corresponding props. Label each bin with the name of the book and organize them in a way that makes sense for you (alphabetically, by theme, by genre, and so forth). If you don't have a storage space in your room, work with a colleague to find space in a bookroom, library, closet, or other logical location. By doing this, you might wind up with a partner who will not only share the lit kits with you, but who will also help you create and maintain them. If you each create 20 kits, you could introduce a new one weekly for a whole school year!

If you store kits in a common area for multiple users, create a sign-up sheet that requires users to reserve particular kits for particular dates or simply ask them to put a post-it note on a kit that they hope to use on a particular date. What's most important is communicating with your colleagues to create the best kits possible—and avoid conflicts when it comes to using them.

Instead of using plastic bins, this teacher uses pizza boxes to store her kits. This system works especially well for oversized books.

Nothing beats the durability of sturdy plastic bins. Transparent bins allow you to see the contents without having to remove the kit.

Concluding Thoughts

For many teachers, dramatic play conjures up thoughts of multiple children in a dress-up area, using large, elaborate props. Literacy kits allow children to explore fiction and nonfiction on a smaller, though no less valuable, scale. Through their play, they can reenact stories, take on characters' roles, and compare objects and texts to unveil the mysteries of nature. In the process, they gain important comprehension and vocabulary skills. And have fun while they're at it!

Chapter 3

Puppets and Flannel Boards

From Howdy Doody to Lamb Chop to Kermit the Frog, some puppets are the rock stars of the toy world. We've all enjoyed their magic. However, as entertaining as puppets may be, we might not think of them as a tool for promoting children's literacy. The fact is, though, playing with puppets and watching puppet shows can help develop children's language and storytelling skills. In this chapter, I talk about literacy-boosting ways to use puppets and their instructional cousins, flannel boards.

How Do Puppets Promote Literacy?

Puppets can be marvelously versatile. They enable children to tell stories they have heard before and to make up brand new stories. Children might use commercially made puppets designed to go with a particular book, such as the finger puppets that accompany Don and Audrey Wood's *Piggies*, and then reenact the story. From there, they might make up their own stories, using the same puppets. More generic puppets, such as a princess, prince, and dragon, offer the chance for children to reenact a variety of stories such as *Sleeping Beauty*, *The Paper Bag Princess*, and *Alexander and the Dragon*—or to go off in a direction all their own.

You may want to capture children's stories on paper by either taking dictation from them or having the children themselves draw what happens. This builds understanding of how stories work: that there's a beginning, middle, and end; that adding details makes for a better story; that characters within and among stories behave and speak in different ways; and so forth.

When children tell or retell a story using puppets, they must express themselves from the point of view of one character. By deciding what kind of voice the character will have, what the character will do, and how the character will act, the child shows her understanding of the story—and her grasp of the concept of

Commercially made puppets can help children bring beloved picture books to life.

Piggies

AUDREY WOOD   DON WOOD

character. Taking dictation, encouraging drawing, and asking for tellings and retellings will serve children well when formal reading and writing instruction is introduced later.

Puppets can be especially helpful to children who are experiencing language delays, are learning English, and/or are intimidated to talk in front of others because the puppets provide a safe level of distance and anonymity. Allowing these children to perform at a puppet stage can make them feel even more secure.

This little girl had trouble speaking up until she put a puppet on her hand. Then she lit up and performed a whole show—in Japanese!

Types of Puppets

There are all kinds of puppets out there. As I mentioned, there are commercially made puppets based on standard storybook characters such as kings, witches, fairies, dragons, and any animal you can imagine. There are also puppets based on favorite storybook characters, such as Winnie the Pooh and Clifford.

Handmade Puppets

Sometimes, the best types of puppets are those children create themselves. As children choose and assemble materials, they must think about essential literacy-related matters, such as how the puppet will look, what the puppet will say, when the puppet will appear in the show and for what reason. Here are some easy puppets for children to make:

Stick puppet: Have children draw pictures of characters from a story that they tell you or that you've read together. Cut out the character and glue it to a tongue depressor or craft stick.

Spoon puppet: Have children decorate a wooden spoon with a face and hair, using markers, pipe cleaners, yarn, ribbon, and other everyday materials.

Paper-bag puppet: Have children use fabric, ribbon, googly eyes, paint, markers, glitter, and so forth to decorate a paper lunch bag, reserving the bag's fold for the mouth.

Sock puppet: Have children draw or affix eyes to the heel of a clean, child-sized sock. From there, have them insert a hand into the sock and tuck the toe into their palm to make a mouth. Adding lips, a tongue, and yarn hair can make the puppet even more convincing.

Finger Puppets

As you build a collection of puppets, consider finger puppets as well as hand puppets. That way, puppet shows needn't require several children. Just a couple of children can take on multiple roles. Also, finger puppets are perfect for table-top play, in case you'd rather not deal with a large stage. Children can easily make finger puppets when you provide them with the "fingers" cut from old gloves. They can decorate them as they would the puppets listed above.

Hand Puppets

Adult-sized hand puppets can be difficult for young children to manipulate. So snag child-sized puppets whenever possible. (One year, a parent of one of my students made a lovely collection of child-sized felt puppets for our class. She used her own child's hand as a template.) You might want to set aside some puppets for your use exclusively and some for the children's. For example, I had a pair of monkey puppets that I used only for social problem solving activities. Because they weren't stored with all the other puppets, the children knew something special was going to happen when they came out. Holding some resources in reserve increases their WOW factor.

Whether you're using hand puppets or finger puppets, have a balance of human and animal characters to maximize the number of stories students can tell or retell. A few based on popular characters from published stories is fine, but most puppets should be based on generic characters to encourage children to make up their own stories and not rely solely on those they've heard.

Types of Puppet Stages

Puppet stages can take many forms, from simple to sophisticated. Regardless of the type of stage children are using, puppet play gives them rich opportunities to retell published stories or tell their own stories.

Tabletop stage

Commercially made stage

Over-the-sofa stage

Outdoor stage

JoDell Warren

Puppets or Boxing Gloves?

Puppets can enliven the classroom. Some teachers, though, hesitate to use them because they may encourage aggressive behavior. Children might use them as boxing gloves. But taking a moment to introduce the puppets and discuss how to play with them appropriately can make a big difference. Keep in mind, many children, especially very young children, don't get that a person makes a puppet talk. Many of them think the puppet is real and, therefore, in control of its own behavior, for better or worse. To help those children, follow these steps:

These children are learning appropriate puppet play by using puppets for their intended purpose—as characters.

1. Have each child select a puppet from a collection that you assemble beforehand.

2. Have children lay their puppet on the floor in front of themselves.

3. Have them decide on a name for their puppet.

4. Have them think about the kind of voice the puppet should have.

5. Have them put the puppet on their hand and say, in their chosen voice, "Hello, my name is _____" to the child sitting next to them.

6. To prevent distraction, have them put their puppet hand behind their backs. Put your puppet behind your back.

7. Ask the children to think of what their puppet likes to do for fun.

8. Ask them to have their puppet tell the child sitting next to them what he or she likes to do for fun.

9. Have the children put their puppet hand behind their backs again.

10. Using their puppet's voice, have them ask their classmate what they like to eat. Tell them to answer when they are asked!

11. Using their puppet's voice, have them tell their classmate a story about something that happened to them.

Keep doing this kind of supported talking until you're confident that children can do it on their own. If you have an especially physical group, consider doing this activity with finger puppets before trying it with hand puppets. That way, if someone gets physical, he or she will use just one finger rather than a fist.

Before setting children loose with the puppets, consider establishing rules with them. Your conversation might start like this:

> "Sometimes, children use puppets in ways that can hurt other children or the puppets. What do you think we should do if someone uses the puppets in a way that is inappropriate?" [Listen and reflect on their ideas.]

> "What do you think we could do with the puppets?" [Make a list of suggestions for constructive use. Post it near the puppet area or stage.]

> "How many people should be in the puppet area or stage at a time?" [Make a sign indicating how many children are allowed at once.]

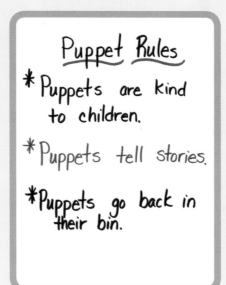

Rules for puppet play

A sign indicating the number of children who can play at one time

If children use the materials inappropriately, refer them to the list of constructive uses. Keep in mind that "misbehavior" is often the result of "miscommunication" about expectations. Give children the chance to behave appropriately by telling them what "appropriate behavior" is. . . and isn't.

What Is a Flannel Board?

Another way to encourage storytelling and retelling is by using flannel boards—a fabric-covered surface children use to attach and manipulate felt cut-outs of characters and objects from the story. Commercial flannel boards are available through most early childhood supply catalogs, but many teachers create their own simply by slipping a board into a flannel pillow case or stapling flannel to a thick piece of cardboard. Both options work well. The point is to create a surface on which felt pieces can be placed to illustrate a story as it is being told.

Flannel board pieces are also available commercially. They are often sold in sets based on particular stories or nursery rhymes, such as "Little Miss Muffet" and concepts, such as healthy foods. Online sources include www.feltsource.com, www.funfelt.com, and www.feltboardstories.com. Occasionally, sets based on stories and nursery rhymes are sold with the book.

You can make pieces easily as well. I'm always dazzled when teachers show me sets they have created by tracing illustrations in a book onto Pellon interfacing (which is available in fabric stores) and then coloring them and cutting them out. Other teachers have created pieces either by drawing on felt or sewing together pieces of felt, using resources such as Liz and Dick Wilmes *Feltboard Fingerplays* for patterns.

This is a homemade flannel board. To create the board, teachers simply clip a piece of flannel onto the easel when needed. Here, those teachers extend ideas from *Mouse Count* to build basic math skills.

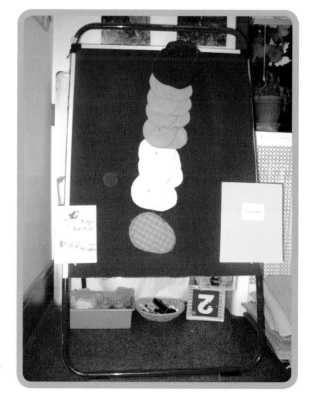

This is a commercially made flannel board. The pieces for the story, *Caps for Sale*, were created with two purposes in mind: for children to retell the story on the flannel board and to wear, if they choose to act out the retelling.

I have never had the talent, patience, or time to do that. Instead, I've cut out illustrations from dog-earred editions of favorite books, laminated them, and glued felt onto the back. I have since met teachers who use either adhesive-backed felt (which is available in craft stores) or Velcro on the backs of the pieces. These are just a few inexpensive options for building a large collection of flannel board sets.

A flannel board need not be a board at all.
In this case, it's an apron!

Storing Flannel Board Sets

Storing your sets is simple. Some teachers place pieces in a pocketed folder, label the folder with the book that inspired the set, and store the folders in a magazine case in the library, with a general-purpose flannel board nearby. Other teachers create folders with flannel boards built in. They adhere felt on the inside right of a file folder, staple a zippered plastic bag containing the pieces to the inside left, and store the book that inspired the set inside the folder. Folders are stored in a file box or a file cabinet.

You can make book-specific flannel board sets easily, using file folders. Choose books, create pieces from felt, store pieces in a zippered plastic bag, and use a magazine case to hold the folders.

38

How to Use a Flannel Board

Flannel boards can be used by you during large- or small-group time, by children during choice time, or by children and their parents at home. They can be used to teach math (sorting shapes, recognizing numerals), science (discussing animals and their habitats, reporting the weather), or social studies (things in the city/things in the country). For the purposes of this book, I'll focus on incorporating them into literacy instruction.

Malinda Merrill

For Retelling Stories

The concrete, tactile nature of flannel-board play makes it perfect for retelling stories. When you ask for a retelling, encourage children not only to manipulate the pieces, but also to refer to the book (especially if their memory starts breaking down). Ask them questions such as, "How does the story start?" "Then what happened?" "Then what?" and finally, "How does the story end?" By using the book as a reference, children can confirm what happens and include more details.

Revisiting Retelling

Retelling—reading or hearing a text and telling it back in one's own words—is an important strategy for promoting children's comprehension. (Morrow, 1985). To do a detailed retelling, children need to understand the story's sequence, important vocabulary, characters, and key events, and be able to wrap up their retelling with an ending that makes sense. This can be challenging for some children. Repeated readings of the text can help. Letting children place the flannel pieces on the board while listening to the story can too.

For Clarifying Concepts

In Pat Hutchins's *The Doorbell Rang*, a group of children learn an important, but discouraging lesson about math. At the start of the story, the children have plenty of cookies—but as the doorbell starts ringing and the guests start arriving, their cookie supply starts dwindling. The more guests they receive, the fewer cookies they have. This concept is abstract for many children. But by using a flannel board to show a large plate filled with all the cookies and then dividing those cookies onto smaller plates as you read the story, it becomes evident that when the doorbell rings, the number of cookies on the large plate decreases. The abstract becomes concrete by manipulating the pieces on a flannel board. . . something that can't be done with a book alone.

For Discussing Informational Text

We know that children enjoy information books. We also know that retelling doesn't work the same way for those books as it does for stories. Often informational books don't have a clear beginning, middle, and end in the way that stories do. Instead, they might contain a collection of interesting facts on a topic, organized chronologically, numerically, or thematically. It's not uncommon for a

Malinda Merrill

retelling of an information book to look and sound like a list of interrelated facts. For example, after reading or hearing a book about pond life, a child may retell the text this way, using the flannel board:

Ponds have water.
[Place a blue shape on the board.]

Ponds have weeds.
[Place clumps of cattails around pond.]

Ducks live on ponds.
[Place a duck on the pond.]

Frogs live in ponds.
[Place frogs on the pond.]

Fish live in ponds.
[Place fish in the pond.]

Be sure to discuss the concepts with the children before, during, and after the retelling. Also, as with the retelling of a story, children are more likely to add details to the retelling of an informational text when they are allowed to consult that text.

Selecting Books for Flannel-Board Activities

Nearly any story can be captured on a flannel board. But, in my experience, those that meet the following criteria are best:

- Books that are familiar, such as *The Three Billy Goats Gruff* by Paul Galdone

- Books that are based on songs, such as Raffi's *Everything Grows*, or nursery rhymes, such as "Little Boy Blue" and "Jack and Jill Went Up the Hill"

- Books that have a simple story line, such as Esphyr Slobodkina's *Caps for Sale*

- Books in which sequence is inconsequential to maximize the number of characters and events the child remembers. If we ask for a retelling of a book such as *Snowballs* by Lois Ehlert, for example, knowing that the "snow dad" was created before the "snow cat" isn't as important as knowing that those two things were created, plain and simple, along with many other characters. The order is less important than the content itself, in other words.

Here are a few other examples that have worked especially well for me:

The Big Red Barn by Margaret Wise Brown

Brown Bear, Brown Bear, What Do You See? by Bill Martin, Jr. and Eric Carle

Brown Rabbit's Shape Book by Alan Baker

The Catalog by Jasper Tomkins

Dinosaurs, Dinosaurs by Byron Barton

The Doorbell Rang by Pat Hutchins

Down by the Bay by Raffi

Elmer by David McKee

Freight Train by Donald Crews

Goldilocks and the Three Bears by James Marshall

Honey. . . Honey. . . Lion! by Jan Brett

I Know an Old Lady (multiple versions available)

Is Your Mama a Llama? by Deborah Guarino

It Looked Like Spilt Milk by Charles G. Shaw

Selecting Books for Flannel-Board Activities continued

Mouse Magic by Ellen Stoll Walsh

One, Two, One Pair by Bruce McMillan

Over in the Meadow by Ezra Jack Keats

Snowballs by Lois Ehlert

The Snowy Day by Ezra Jack Keats

Swimmy by Leo Lionni

The Three Little Pigs (multiple versions available)

The Three Little Wolves and the Big Bad Pig by Eugene Trivizas

Who's in Rabbit's House? by Verna Aardema

For Extending Literacy Development at Home

Send home a flannel board, its accompanying pieces, and a book, just as you might send home a library book. Let families know what the set is for and how to use it. Encourage family members to read the book, talk about the story, and have the child retell the story using the flannel board pieces. Doing this puts a fun, new spin on traditional bedtime reading.

Concluding Thoughts

Connecting to text is what comprehension is all about. By using dramatic play to help children make sense of a story or informational text, we increase their odds of becoming proficient readers and writers down the road. Puppets and flannel boards are useful in helping children make connections because they require them to retell familiar stories or tell stories of their own. Informational text comes alive as children manipulate pieces, recall facts, and make connections between and among concepts. For most children, puppets and flannel boards are effective tools for finding their voices as they make sense of texts and text structures.

Chapter 4

Prop Boxes

As teachers, we need to accomplish so much in so little time. Wouldn't it be great if we could walk into our classrooms, lay our hands on the materials we need, and quickly create experiences that broaden children's literacy knowledge, deepen their world knowledge, and invite imaginary play? We can! Prop boxes can help us achieve all of those things, if we design and use them carefully.

What Is a Prop Box?

A prop box is a collection of materials that enhance children's dramatic play. Typically stored in a large box or plastic tub, the materials are organized by theme such as "restaurant," "airplane," and "castle," and fall into two categories:

1. theme-related props from the real world to enrich the play and make it more authentic, such as play food, tableware, pans, cash register, aprons, centerpiece, and placemats

2. print-rich materials to enrich children's interactions with text, such as a chart with the evening's specials, menus, a cookbook, recipe cards, an order pad, and a dessert list

For a complete list of themes, theme-related props, and print-rich materials, see pages 46–50.

Unlike lit kits, puppets, and flannel boards, prop boxes invite children to create whole worlds, take on roles, and act and interact within those worlds. The role-playing that prop boxes invite helps children develop the cognitive, linguistic, and social skills necessary to function in particular, real-world situations. It allows them to make sense of those situations on their own terms, using appropriate vocabulary, creating stories on the spot and re-enacting ones they've heard, and working through conflicts and finding solutions. In this way, children gain important life skills, as well as important vocabulary and comprehension skills that will come in handy later, when they're learning to read and write (Neuman & Roskos, 1993).

What Does a Prop Box Contain?

Deciding what to include in a prop box is usually pretty straightforward. For example, if you were to create a restaurant, you'd undoubtedly need a table, chairs and menus. But don't be afraid to tap your creativity by also including aprons,

order pads, fancy dress-up clothes, and a picture cookbook. Think about your theme. What do you want children to learn about? What do you want children to be able to do? The box "Things to Consider When Choosing Materials for Prop Boxes" on the next page should guide your thinking.

Things to Consider When Choosing Materials for Prop Boxes

Prop boxes have been shown to enhance children's literacy skills (Neuman & Roskos, 1993). Once you've come up with a theme, think about the following criteria as you choose materials for the box.

Appropriateness	• Are the materials safe for the children with whom you work? (Avoid using items that might be construed as dangerous, such as glass mirrors, plastic bags, and lead pencils.) • Do the materials support your theme? • Can children identify the theme just by looking at the materials?
Authenticity	• Would a child find the materials in the real world? • Can you locate a source of "real" materials, such as menus from an actual restaurant or message pads from an office?
Creativity	• Can the materials be used in a variety of ways? • Are there ways that the children can contribute materials to the box? Could they create some themselves? • Do you have a variety of prop boxes to attract different children? For example, some children will never go into "housekeeping" but may be very attracted to a bakery (similar but different themes). • Do you have a variety of materials in each prop box to attract different children? For example, in a fire station prop box, you might include not only firefighter hats and hoses, but also dolls and a typewriter to appeal to a wide range of children.
Connectedness to Text	• Are the materials connected to a book or song that you have used? Can you provide a copy of that text in the box? (Keep in mind that not all texts are books. Some are lists, menus, songs, and so forth.) • Have you read related texts to the children or will you provide them with texts they might use in the center on their own (such as a guide book for a campout)? If you include a reference book, do you plan to spend time helping children use it? • If the text is environmental (such as ice cream parlor signs), how will you help children read and make sense of it?
Usefulness	• Will the children actually use the materials? Do they need a demonstration?
Variety	• Do you have enough boxes to change your theme every week or so? (Some teachers leave materials out longer than a week because the children don't come every day or because they observe continued interest in the theme.) • Are you embracing a range of themes that will appeal to all your children over time? For example, having only transportation-related themes, such as *boat*, *airplane*, or *submarine*, may appeal to some children but not to others. Conversely, service-related themes, such as *hospital*, *housekeeping*, and *vet clinic*, may appeal to a completely different group. Select and vary themes to cover all your children's interests.

Themes, Theme-Related Props, and Print-Rich Materials

Themes and Theme-Related Props	Print-Rich Materials
Airplane: windows that look out onto clouds, chairs in rows, "cockpit" separated from main part of plane by refrigerator and stove, headsets for pilots, steering wheel for pilot and co-pilot (can be just circles of cardboard affixed to box with brads), small overnight suitcases with dress-up clothes, pretend food and dishes	travel brochures (available for free from travel agencies), maps, flight manual (real or made up), order pad and pencils for flight attendants, advertising posters with slogans like "Fly the friendly skies," flight safety cards, in-flight magazines (available from airlines), nametags, tickets, passports
Bakery: flour in texture table, natural colored play dough (and tons of it!), cookie cutters, rolling pins, pans, oven, sink, aprons, oven mitts, phone, cash register, money, boxes decorated to look like cakes	bakery sign, price lists, labels on shelves of baked goods, order forms, pencils, recipe cards, cookbook, paper for children to label their creations
Boat: tape shape of boat onto the floor, with kitchen area (galley), chairs for fishing, fishing poles, life jackets, binoculars, plastic bugs and worms for bait	maps of lakes, fish field guides, posters of different types of fish, fishing magazines, *Ranger Rick*, *Big Backyard*, and *Wild Animal Baby* magazines, "Watch your step!" sign, labels for starboard/port
Book Shop: cash register, money, display racks, bean bag or other comfortable chairs, cups for hot chocolate, mock pastries/cookies	book posters, wide range of books including child-made books, magazines, book marks, signs indicating sales and author readings
Campsite: tent, stuffed animals, plastic bugs, binoculars, pretend fire, play food, dishes, small picnic table, sleeping bags, fishing poles, backpacks	wildlife posters (available for free from your state's department of natural resources), field guides or books on birds (or mammals, dinosaurs, etc., depending on the theme), camp cookbook
Castle: cardboard castle (refrigerator box opened up with top cut like a crenellated top), princess clothes, knight costumes, crowns, fairy costumes, brass goblets, fancy table cloths, food, fireplace for cooking, pots, cloaks, aprons, musical instruments for minstrels	scrolls, quill and "ink" (feather and paint), parchment (tan colored paper with edges torn), posters of castle life or clothes, maps, tapestries with text, music for minstrels to play

Campsite

Children use a campsite prop box to explore the great outdoors within and beyond the classroom. The box includes props for camping, such as a pretend campfire, sticks and "marshmallows" (cotton balls), fishing poles, and backpacks, as well as print-rich materials such as hiking guides, magazines on local wildlife, books on tracking animals, and maps of the area.

Themes and Theme-Related Props	Print-Rich Materials
Firehouse: phone, hoses, fire truck created from box, climber or lined up chairs, coats, rubber boots, fire hats, extinguisher (can be an oatmeal canister covered in red paper with piece of hose attached)	map of city, poster of the order in which to put on gear, fire safety posters, paper and pencil for taking phone messages
Flower Shop: texture table with potting soil, plastic pots, artificial flowers, phone, cash register, money, shovels, plastic vases, refrigerator for floral arrangements, ribbon	seed packets with labels, posters of plants, FTD book (get an old one from your local florist), FTD calendar (free from florist), sticks with names of plants on them, order forms and pencils, small note cards to place in bouquet
Grocery Store: tables, small grocery carts, cash register, money, purses, wallets, brown paper bags (not plastic bags for safety reasons)	signs for shelves, coupons, grocery store ads from paper, posters of different foods, empty containers of foods or other products donated by families, sale posters
Housekeeping: stove, refrigerator, babies, chairs and tables, dishes, baby supplies, mailbox	newspapers, children's books, baby/parenting magazines, paper and pencils, shopping ads, slim paper for list making, coupons, magnetic letters for fridge, signs like "There's no place like home," and "Welcome," photo albums with captions, letters in mailbox
Ice Cream Parlor: dishes, cones made from paper, spoons, table and chairs, tubs of "ice cream" (yarn pompoms in a variety of colors, or Styrofoam balls painted in a variety of colors, some with circles of Velcro to make double dip cones by stacking balls), ice cream scoops, money, cash register, aprons	order forms and pencils, poster of flavor choices, price poster, store sign, labels on flavor buckets, empty containers of chocolate sauce, butterscotch or cherry toppings
Music Store: musical instruments, microphone, stage, cash register, money, mirror, costumes	tape recorder, sheet music, signs for instruments, sale signs, posters of instruments, posters of musicians, records/CDs

Firehouse

After inviting the children to create a fire truck from a large cardboard box, the teachers transform the dramatic-play area into a firehouse. The children use housekeeping props and materials to prepare food while waiting for a fire call; when the call comes, they quickly don their uniforms and refer to a city map to locate the fire.

Themes and Theme-Related Props	Print-Rich Materials
Photography Studio: cameras, dress-up clothes (as glamorous as possible!), cash register, money, stuffed animals, chair, silk flowers	price lists with poses and labels of options (standing, sitting, with pet, two people, etc.), greeting cards with pictures, posters from photo shops for film or photo packages
Pizza Parlor: felt circles of white and red to make pizza and sauce, felt toppings like cheese, pepperoni, mushrooms, green pepper (each in their own container for sorting), oven, oven mitts, phone, cash register, money, table for eating "in," dishes, apron	order forms, pencils, pizza cookbook, menus, signs advertising the daily special, posters of pizza or scenes from Italy
Post Office: mailbox, bags for delivery, hats for letter carriers (or plastic visors since they are easily sanitized), bin for packages and mail labeled "US Postal Service," scale for weighing letters, tape for wrapping packages	packages with labels, letters, envelopes, stampers and pads, stickers such as those that come from junk mail, mailbox sorting bin (use a shoe sorter if mailboxes aren't available), posters for stamps, price lists for mailing, zip codes for local communities
Restaurant: play food, aprons, chef hat, dishes, vase with flowers, tables set for dining, money, cash register, dress up clothes	menus, cookbooks, signs for restaurant, chalkboard or dry erase board for "specials," order pads and pencils
Submarine: large piece of cardboard (appliance box cut open) with portholes cut in side, steering wheel, periscope, pictures of fish or other underwater creatures, blue tulle or crepe paper draped from ceiling, green crepe paper draped from ceiling for seaweed, diving masks, flippers	guide books on fish, informational books on underwater life such as *Under the Sea* (Delafosse & Gallimard, 1999), posters with text about life underwater
Veterinary Clinic: stuffed animals, medical equipment like stethoscopes, gauze, shotters (without needles!), white doctor coats or adult small white dress shirts	charts of animals, books on animals like DK's book *Dogs* (2005) or *Cats* (2003), pet care books, magazines for the waiting room area, boxes (not bottles) labeled with "medicine" labels, appointment book, medical charts, file folders with paper and pencil

Ice Cream Parlor

This ice cream parlor encourages children to assume all kinds of roles, from customer to clerk. When children seem uncertain about selecting a role and beginning the play, a teacher assists them. Books about ice cream parlors are also included so children can get ideas from them as well.

"Ewww! The Hats Are Moving!" Banning Unwanted "Guests" from Dramatic Play

I recently learned of an excellent local program that doesn't have a dress-up area because the teachers are worried about the spread of lice from sharing hats. While I sympathize, I also regret everything the children are missing. There are precautions we can take to avoid the spread of lice, parasites, and germs in our classrooms.

1. Wash weekly any clothing the children use—or ask a parent volunteer to wash it.

2. Inspect the clothing between washings. If you detect creepies, bag and remove the entire collection. Wash it in hot water to kill all bugs and eggs.

3. Wipe down props with disinfectant wipes, before returning them to the boxes.

4. Limit your use of cloth hats. Consider instead plastic hats, which are easier to sanitize.

5. Keep an eye out for kids who are scratching, coughing, and/or sneezing excessively and gently bring the matter up with parents. Good health and hygiene must be a top priority.

With forethought and diligence, we can invite children into play without worrying about unwanted guests.

If you work with very young children, ages 1 to 3, you probably notice that in their dramatic play they are more likely to re-enact what they've seen than to create whole-new imaginary experiences. For example, they are more likely to care for babies than blast off to the moon. Therefore, choose themes that are very familiar to them, such as:

- pediatrician's office
- housekeeping
- pet shop
- laundromat
- grocery store

Older children, ages 4 to 6, typically thrive on creating imaginary worlds, based on what they observe, hear, discuss, and read about in everyday life. For example, visiting the NASA Web site, exploring books by Seymour Simon, engaging in a class discussion about the first moon landing, and even riding on a plane or bus will undoubtedly inform and enhance their role as astronaut. Consider these themes for them:

- spaceship
- pirate ship
- paleontological dig
- television station
- barn/farm

The key to success is tapping into children's interests and using those interests to design play experiences. You may have a child that is absolutely crazy about block building—so crazy about it, he never leaves the block area. Creating a railroad station prop box might be just the thing to lure that child from the block area into the dress-up area, where he might load the train according to the bill of lading, check the cargo, ensure the train leaves on time, consult a map to assist a passenger, offer a passenger something to read, *and* drive the train. That kind of rich play is very different from simply pushing around a toy train for an hour!

This drawing was inspired by two children's dramatic play. The joy, energy, and imagination are undeniable.

"What's This For?" Building Genre Awareness With Real-World Materials

Did you ever notice that children know the conventions of various kinds of texts before they're even able to write those texts? For example, they know personal letters often begin with "Dear" and stories often begin with "Once upon a time. . ." This doesn't happen by accident. When children are exposed to a variety of texts, they come to understand the differences between those texts.

This kind of genre awareness is important to children's emerging ability to comprehend text. Children need to understand that some texts are linear, such as a story or a letter, and some are non-linear, such as a field guide and a restaurant menu.

It is also important to children's emerging writing skills. Even first graders can produce texts that contain features of specific genres (Duke & Bennett-Armistead, 2003). For example, they might include a caption under a picture they draw. They might begin a story with "once upon a time. . ." and end it with ". . . and they all lived happily ever after," of course, using invented spelling. That awareness comes from being exposed to a variety of genres *before* they are asked to produce them.

By offering print-rich materials in prop boxes, you build genre awareness playfully. The grocery store has coupons; the doctor's office has an appointment book and prescriptions; the library has check-out cards to stamp; the post office has letters to mail. Each "location" offers a different genre to get to know.

Your Role in Promoting Rich Play

Even the most imaginative children benefit from having adults interact with them as they play. Here's what you can do to ensure that children get the most out of prop boxes:

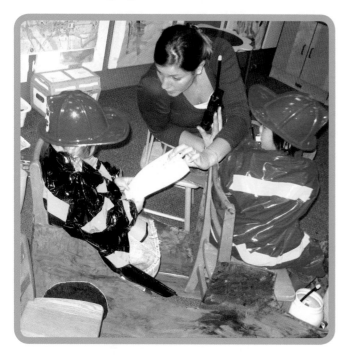

Adults play several key roles in promoting children's play and their connection to text through play. This teacher, for example, is pointing out the importance of checking a map for the location of a fire *before* racing to put it out.

- Introduce materials so children know what to do with them. "This is a periscope. They use these on submarines to look out the top of the submarine and see what's on top of the water."

- When children are "stuck," suggest a new direction for their play. For example, if children are playing bakery and making only cookies, you might say, "Hi, I'd like to order a wedding cake. Can I tell you what kind of cake I want? Can you draw me a picture of what you think it will look like?"

- Help reluctant or resistant children join in. For example, you might notice that Damien is just watching while JeQuan is actively playing. You could say, "JeQuan, it looks like you're the cook. You need someone to eat all that food. Should Damien be the customer or the waiter?"

- Introduce new vocabulary for use in the play. For example, while playing in the photography studio, you might say, "When you take the picture, look through the *lens* to see what the shot will look like."

- Demonstrate ways to use materials that children may not think of on their own. For example, "Wow, we better radio in to the fire station to let them know the emergency is under control!" or "Let's raise the Jolly Roger so other sailors know this is a pirate ship."

Observing children reveals important clues about what you can do to enrich the play. A good general rule is "follow the children." Acknowledge what they're doing and, without orchestrating the play, add a new twist to build upon it in a constructive way.

Prop Box Storage

Many teachers I know use cardboard boxes for storing prop box materials because they are free, easy to label, and easy to stack. They tend to get raggedy, though, in a short time. So at my school, we use plastic bins. I must confess I prefer the look and "stackability" of matching bins, but we live with donated, mismatched bins for cost reasons. When I ran the lab school at Michigan State University, we used

Using a common storage space for prop boxes allows all teachers to have access them. Labeling the boxes makes for easy retrieval.

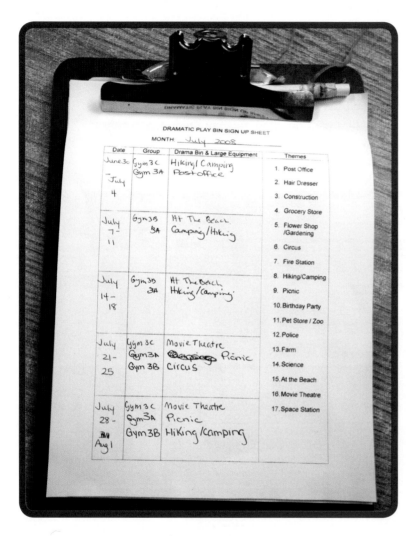

an old bureau, designating a drawer to each theme. On a rack above the bureau we hung clothing that was used for a variety of themes. We stored the bureau and rack in a clean, dry basement room that all teachers could access. Other teachers I know use outside storage sheds, attic space, cellar space, and even a space in the lead teacher's garage. If prop boxes are important to you, you'll find a place for them.

To avoid conflicts, teachers in this program sign up in advance for the prop box they'd like to use in a given week. The clipboard is stored near the boxes so the teachers know what is available and isn't, at a glance.

Concluding Thoughts

Prop boxes expose children to literacy materials that they might not otherwise use and create a foundation of knowledge that children can draw upon in their writing and reading now and in years to come. For you, the teacher, they provide a quick and easy way to implement rich, thematic play experiences, day to day, week to week.

Chapter 5

Theme Trunks

During a recent trip to Hamilton, Ontario, I visited an incredible classroom where children were engaged in literacy activities all over the room. I saw children in costumes acting out *The Three Little Pigs*, other children making pig snouts to wear at their performance, stories the children had written about farm animals, and a rebus version of *The Three Little Pigs* that the children had dictated to the teachers. Everywhere, children were engaged in looking at, creating, or using text. It was inspiring. To make all this happen, the teachers in Hamilton were using "theme trunks," which they borrowed from the local children's agency that created them.

What Is a Theme Trunk?

A theme trunk is sort of a super-sized, combined lit kit and prop box. Like a lit kit, it is literature focused. Like a prop box, it contains themed costumes and props. However, unlike a lit kit or prop box, a theme-trunk is designed to support play based on multiple, related texts. For example, the materials for *The Three Little Pigs* activities described on the previous page were part of a trunk called Classic Tales, which also included materials for *Goldilocks and the Three Bears* and *Little Red Riding Hood.*

The Hamilton teachers used the funds from a grant to hire a gifted costume designer to create beautiful child-sized costumes. If hiring a designer is cost prohibitive, see Chapter 6 for suggestions on locating props and costumes. Commercial or child-produced materials can work just as well in supporting children's creative play.

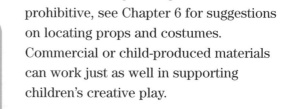

Theme Trunk Storage

The Hamilton teachers use steamer trunks to store theme trunk materials. A tray inside the trunk holds the collection of books. The trunk's main compartment is used to store costumes and props.

But you need not use trunks. For example, throughout this chapter you'll notice pictures of "trunks" that are actually suitcases or other containers. Whatever you have that is large enough to hold your collection is fine.

Color coding trunks makes it easy
to find just the one you're looking for.

Storing trunks (or anything else!) is always a challenge. You might decide, as the folks in Ontario did, to have a central location that many classrooms access for storage. This might be in a local agency office, your program's administrative offices, or just the basement of your building. You might decide instead, as I did with some colleagues years ago, that each of you will keep one trunk in your own classroom storage area and then share and shift them as needed.

How to Use a Theme Trunk

Because trunks typically contain a wide variety of materials, you can pick and choose items that best suit your goals. For example, the class described on page 57 was immersed in a theme unit on farms. From the trunk, the teacher used only materials related to *The Three Little Pigs*.

In addition to *The Three Little Pigs*, she read aloud *The Three Little Wolves and the Big Bad Pig* and had the class compare the two books. As a follow up, the students retold *The Three Little Pigs* by creating and illustrating a rebus version of it.

A rebus version of *The Three Little Pigs*, created by the teachers and the children.

The class also researched the names of baby animals, hatched chicks and documented their growth, created papier maché farm animals, wrote about animals they'd like to be, made their own pig snouts and, as already mentioned, acted out the story in rich detail while wearing pig and wolf costumes from the trunk. The theme trunk enriched an already literacy-rich classroom, allowing the children to make the stories their own.

Student-made pig snouts

Papier maché farm animals

In short, theme trunks offer a wide array of books, costumes, and props that support a primary theme, as well as several secondary themes. The teachers report that theme trunks not only spur the children's creativity, but their own as well.

Themes to Consider for Trunks

For toddlers and preschoolers:

- Classic Tales
- Castles and Fairy Tales
- Ocean
- Forest Animals
- Farm
- Authors (such as Eric Carle, Dr. Seuss, and Margaret Wise Brown)
- Heros and Heroines (includes community helpers)
- Nursery Rhymes
- Transportation
- Science Campouts (includes entomology, paleontology, geology, ornithology, botany)

Especially good for toddlers:

- Baby Care
- Pets
- Transportation
- Medical Center

Especially good for older preschoolers:

- Wizards/Magic
- Growing Things
- Talent Show (including microphones and a stage)

What Does a Theme Trunk Contain?

In addition to a large collection of fiction and nonfiction books on a specific theme (for suggested titles, see appendix), theme trunks may contain suggestions for literacy-rich activities, a wide array of store-bought and handmade props and costumes to act out stories, and the kind of print-rich materials found in prop boxes. For example, the pirate kit includes treasure maps and a captain's log.

Each trunk is a bit different. The Wizards trunk, for example, is designed for school-age children and includes the Harry Potter series and books on magic tricks. Rather than storing materials in a single trunk, the teachers store them in well-traveled suitcases. The suitcases themselves can be used as props.

The books and props for the Pirates trunk
are stored in an old treasure-style chest, with
costumes stored in a separate garment bag.

Children can dress up. . .

search for treasure. . .

and interact with books on pirates and write about pirates, if they choose.

Each trunk also includes a scrapbook that borrowers fill In with photos of children using materials and comments from children about the trunk.

Suggestions for Community Use

As I mentioned earlier, the teachers in Hamilton store the theme trunks in a central location and check them out when they want to use them, typically for about two weeks. Each trunk contains an inventory list so that teachers can check to be sure all materials are accounted for and returned safely.

If your community doesn't have such a collection, consider creating one. Creating one or two trunks will get you started so you can rotate what you have and share with a colleague. If you are part of a director's group or a family day-care consortium, you and other members might decide to share theme trunks. As a group, you would need to decide on a storage location and a borrowing policy and system. Whatever you come up with, you'll enjoy the key benefit of theme trunks—how they allow you to pick and choose materials to carry out your plans for the children.

Concluding Thoughts

However it is developed and managed, a collection of theme trunks offers wonderful opportunities for you and the children to be creative as you promote literacy. You can use them as a centerpiece for your instruction or you can pick and choose from the contents to enrich an already rich theme. The use and management options are limited only by your imagination. The benefits to children are limitless!

Chapter 6

Setting Up and Managing Dramatic Play

If I've done my job as author, I've convinced you that dramatic play is good for kids. But you may be wondering, "How do I make it happen and keep it going?" You may be struggling with the everyday issues of obtaining materials, designing spaces, and managing the play itself. In this chapter, I address:

- Where to locate materials

- How to design space for dramatic play

- How to set limits for successful interaction among children

- How to boost children's interaction with text

"Where the Heck Am I Supposed to Get All This Stuff?": Locating Materials

As discussed in Chapters 2, 4, and 5, lit kits, prop boxes, and theme trunks can be wonderful resources in any program. The lists on pages 23–27, 46–50, and 62 can help you think through what you might need to create them. The prospect of finding all that stuff, though, can be daunting. So take a multi-pronged approach:

- Reduce, reuse, recycle
- Put the word out
- Consider who might have what you need
- Scavenge for what you need
- Get your children's families in on the hunt
- Make it yourself

Reduce, Reuse, Recycle

As early childhood educators, we are resourceful. We seldom have big budgets and, therefore, make do with what's on hand. When it comes to building lit kits, prop boxes, theme trunks, and the like, our resourcefulness can be a real boon. Look around at what you have and think of new ways to use it. For example, say your space ship needs a control panel. Might you create one by drawing knobs on an upside-down cardboard box and attaching the headsets from the listening center? Could you use that old boom box in the back room as the radio for contacting Mission Control? Most everyone has a broken or outdated computer somewhere. What new purpose might it serve? Creative problem solving can be a lifesaver. Just be sure to exercise it sooner rather than later to avoid last-minute brainstorming.

Put the Word Out

This is an old strategy that I apply to most every aspect of my life—whether I'm looking for a reliable babysitter, a trustworthy banker, or a good bagel. But in the case of obtaining classroom materials, I've found it especially invaluable. Let's pretend you're looking for field guides to include in your campsite prop box. Let everyone in your school know. Tell your mom. Put out an email. Mention it to as many people as you can. You never know what they have and would be happy to part with until you ask. In addition to field guides, you may wind up with travel maps, supply checklists, travel brochures, and other forms of print related to camping, not to mention tents, sleeping bags, mess kits, compasses, and so forth.

I once stocked a completely empty classroom this way. Because I let people know what I was looking for, they searched their closets, barns, and bookshelves for materials.

Consider Who Might Have What You Need

Think about the person in your community who would most likely have what you're looking for. For example, imagine you need large-appliance boxes to create a castle. You could drive around your neighborhood on recycling day, hoping to find a few discarded ones, or you could go directly to the source: an appliance store. If you need fine paper to include in your stationery shop, you could buy it at a real stationery shop or you could ask the manager for a donation of discontinued merchandise. Print shops carry high-quality paper as well. Restaurants may give you menus. Ice cream parlors might share cardboard serving bowls, paper hats, promotional signs, and plastic spoons.

In addition to businesses in your community, consider families with children who have outgrown the materials you need. For example, posting a sign at a middle school might yield easels, Legos, baby dolls, kitchen sets, picture books or board books, workbenches, and costumes of all kinds.

Finally, don't forget the school maintenance person. Like no one else, she can locate the unused furniture, holiday decorations, computer hardware, and other essentials for any number of purposes.

Scavenge for What You Need

Scavenging at yard sales, thrift stores, and recycling centers may be off-putting for some, but I must admit, I have had excellent luck locating materials for dramatic play this way. Admittedly, most of the stuff is pretty awful, but from time to time you can find some real gems. And don't forget the old adage, "One person's trash is another's treasure." I once found a clean and fully functional play stove, refrigerator, and washer/dryer set curbside, for instance. As far as I could tell, they were being thrown out just because a child had drawn on them with crayon. So I cleaned them up with a paste made of powdered bathroom cleanser, bleach, and water and restored them to fine condition for my classroom.

In some communities, you'll find open bins for magazines at recycling centers, which provides you with a rich source of print materials on particular themes— fishing, cooking, sports, pet care, and so forth—at no cost. You can use magazines intact or cut them up for activities or for pictures that prompt discussion. A colleague once joyously pulled two years' worth of *Ranger Rick* magazines out of a bin and used them for many themes throughout the year.

Yard sales and thrift stores are especially good for finding dress-up clothes. For example, a woman's petite navy suit can become a police uniform. A white Oxford shirt makes a great lab coat. Large scarves can be used as "raw" material for creating tents, costumes, and blankets. Be creative—and don't disregard potentially popular items too quickly. For example, a lacy peignoir set is not appropriate for small children, but the bed jacket alone might make a lovely princess gown.

Get Your Children's Families in on the Hunt

No one in the community has a greater stake in getting materials for your class than your students' families. So let them know you are actively building a rich collection of dramatic play materials for their children by:

- Sending out a letter asking for donations. (See sample letter on page 71.)

- Including in your weekly newsletter a call for materials as new themes are about to be introduced. This serves a few purposes: you get what you need, you inform families of what you are doing and why, and you give children a first-hand glimpse at how their families support their school. Everybody benefits!

- Calling on specific parents for specific needs. For example, if you know a parent is a doctor, ask her for appropriate medical supplies, discarded instruments, and small-sized scrubs.

Dear Family Member:

We are in the process of developing new dress-up kits for your children to use. We hope to make a number of kits on different themes, for example, a firehouse, a boat, a restaurant, a flower shop, etc. One of our goals in creating these kits is to allow children to learn more about their world by pretending to be in these places. Another goal is to increase children's interaction with print materials that one might find in these places. For example, the boat kit will include fishing or boating magazines, maps of lakes, field guides on fish, a poster about boating safety, instructions on how to drive the boat, and an owner's manual on how to maintain the boat. We're excited about how the kits will help your children grow in their dramatic play and in their literacy.

To create these kits, we need your help. Below are a number of things that you may have at home or that you can secure through friends, family members, discount stores, or yard sales. If you can locate some of these things and would like to donate them, please send them in with your child. You may think of other things that we haven't considered. Please share your ideas with us!

Thank you for your help. The kits will be a wonderful way to enhance your child's play experiences.

Themes we're considering:

housekeeping	firehouse	post office	boat
pirate ship	hospital/vet clinic	grocery store	pizza parlor
restaurant	castle	campsite	music store
ice cream parlor	barn	flower shop	photography studio
submarine	bookstore	train	

Of course, we're open to other ideas if you have them!

Materials we need:

binoculars	field guides	maps	travel brochures
flower catalogues	seed packets	FTD books	plastic vases
plastic flower pots	posters on any topic	picture cookbooks	menus
plastic bugs	small camping gear	small aprons	order pads
appointment books	phones	cash register	typewriter
cameras	play money	coupons	paper grocery bags
silk flowers	magnifying glasses	medical stuff	ace bandages
steering wheel	keyboard	small lab coats	chef's hats
recipe cards	stickers	stamp pads	stampers
backpacks	envelopes	small suitcases	life jackets
felt	plastic worms	costumes	sheet music
headphones			

Your child's teachers

Make It Yourself

Sometimes you just can't locate what you need or you have no budget to purchase it. I had this problem when I wanted cookbooks for a campsite kit. I ended up clipping together illustrations and recipes downloaded from the Internet.

Foil Veggies

1. Wash vegetables.

2. Cut them up.

3. Wrap in aluminum foil.

4. Carefully place into coals of the fire. Let cook for 10 minutes.

5. Remove from fire carefully!

6. Enjoy!

My colleagues and I created a "Camp Cookbook" for children when we couldn't find a commercially published one. Using clip art and real products, such as aluminum foil, make the text come alive for children.

Digital cameras allow us to get creative with class-made books. Try including class-made books into dramatic play. For example, if you go on a field trip to a grocery store, create a photo-filled book based on your trip and make it part of your grocery store prop box. Not only will children enjoy reminiscing about their field trip, they'll get ideas for ways to play in the pretend grocery store.

If you lack the time and/or talent to make what you need, again, consider calling on your families. There may be a creative parent who would love to help—especially a parent who might not be able to help in more traditional ways, such as volunteering his time in the classroom. I had a parent a few years ago who wanted to volunteer, but couldn't because she had a younger child in her care. So she offered to create wonderful props for dramatic play, among other activities, such as child-sized wooden birthday cakes, which she decorated with ceramic "frosting" and drilled with holes for candles. To complete the package, she donated age-specific birthday cards. The children read a card and placed the correct number of candles on the cake. I would have never thought of this on my own. Depending on parents' creativity and generosity ensured that my class had wonderful materials at no cost. If your families are strapped for cash, you might offer to purchase the materials and ask them to do the assembly.

However you gather your materials, your program will benefit from having a rich collection of lit kits, prop boxes, and theme trunks based on your goals and your children's interests.

"Now That I've Got It, Where Do I Put It?": Designing Space for Dramatic Play

If you had to identify what you lack most, like most teachers, you would probably say "money" first and "space" second. Let's face it, early childhood education is a messy business. It requires so many materials. Teachers of school-age children don't need to rotate their materials as frequently as we do. They don't need storage systems as compact and easy to access as ours. They don't need room for their students to play as much as we do. Here, I offer some layout ideas to consider rather than a specific blueprint.

Location, Location, Location

Dramatic play tends to be—and should be—spirited and social. As such, it should be located away from quiet zones such as the reading area and the listening center. At the same time, it should be located close to zones that might inspire "border crossing," in which children take materials from other areas to enhance their play. For example, they may take blocks into the dramatic play area to serve as props in a puppet show. They may compose messages in the writing center and deliver them to the residents of the housekeeping area, or they may make signs for a grocery store. See the floor plan on the next page for one way to organize your room.

This classroom has play areas that are defined well enough so that children know where they begin and end, yet those areas are also open enough to invite literacy-enriching "border crossing."

Consider Interior Layout

If you were redesigning your kitchen at home, you'd need to think about issues such as organization, accessibility, and flow. The same is true for a pretend kitchen at school—or a spaceship, campsite, or grocery store, for that matter. Consider these questions when preparing the space:

- How will the space be used?

- What will the children do?

- What props are needed?

- What print-rich materials are needed?

- How many children does the space need to accommodate?

- How will the set up affect the children's play?

Once you've answered these questions, consider whether the space is large enough or located in the best place. For example, whenever I used a sensory table in my dress-up area for, say, flour for a bakeshop or soil for a flower shop, I moved the dress-up area to

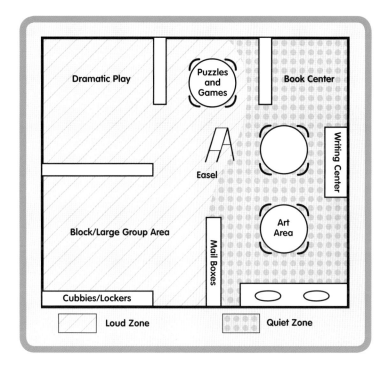

an uncarpeted part of my classroom to make clean up easier. Conversely, during a farm unit, the carpeted floor helped the straw that I had strewn about stay put. Since I didn't have room in my class for two dramatic-play areas, I had to rearrange my space to accommodate the materials and the children. (I was pretty sure the flour would *not* stay in the sensory table!) By creating spaces where children don't have to be hypersensitive about being tidy and safe, we free them to be creative and inventive.

You also need to decide what to do with "extra" equipment—materials you're not using at the moment, but will use later. If you set up a bookstore, for example, what do you do with the refrigerator and stove? If you have the storage, you could put them away while the bookstore is up and running. Since most of us don't have extra space, you could turn them to the wall and use them for bookstore display surfaces. Or you could have two areas: a permanent housekeeping area and a temporary bookstore. This gives children the option of playing house or exploring new ideas in the themed area. Obviously this requires more space, which may not be possible. But if it is possible, try it and see how it works for you.

"How Do I Prevent Chaos?": Setting Limits for Successful Interaction Among Children

When you decide where and what the play will be, set limits in advance to encourage problem solving and discourage inappropriate behavior, such as damaging materials or engaging in aggressive play.

This is a "limit" sign that all children can read because the maximum number of children allowed in the area is depicted with a numeral, a word, and a symbol.

Numbers Game

I am a firm believer in labeling play areas with the maximum number of children allowed at any one time. However, I am *not* a firm believer in zealously enforcing that limit. Essentially the labels encourage children to self-regulate.

Children can go to an area, see that the sign says "4," for example, and count to see if that number has been reached. If it has, they must decide what to do. They can enter the play and run the risk of having someone tattle on them; they can walk away and return later; they can walk away and not return; they can start a wait list; or they can simply play in the area without causing a problem. In other words, by labeling areas this way, we create a text-based problem that children have to work through. So, please, don't use these labels to impose martial law. Instead, use them to support children's developing social and problem-solving skills.

At the beginning of the year, ask children to help you decide how many of them should be allowed to play in each area. Be sure each number is represented as a numeral (4), a word (four), and a visual representation of the number (****). That way, when children ask if they can play in the area, you can reply confidently, "I'm not sure. Did you read the sign?" Let the problem solving begin!

How to Play

Children often use materials in unexpected ways, which can be delightful when, say, cookies become coins or bananas become phones. But what if some children use materials in violent or destructive ways? Decide in advance what is okay and what is not. How do rules for play align with your general class rules? I only had two rules in my classroom: 1) *Take care of people.* 2) *Take care of things.* If a problem arose, I could simply say something like, "Hmmm, if you use that biscuit as a grenade, does that take care of people? I think throwing a grenade in school might hurt people and things." From there, I would redirect the child to a more acceptable activity.

Sometimes, though, stemming inappropriate behavior was not so cut-and-dry. For example, under my rules, gun play was not okay. Consider, then, what you would do with the sweet child of the local minister who, while holding a long block, shouted, "Pow! Pow! Pow!" When I asked what was going on, he stammered, "It's a gu-, a swor-, A HOSE!" My objective was most certainly not to teach children to lie, but that was what he was doing. Nonetheless, I responded, "I'm glad you know that guns aren't a choice," which didn't directly address the larger issue of the child engaging in gun play and then lying about it. I was, however, able to provide a positive reinforcement for appropriate behavior.

This teacher skillfully negotiates a conflict by moving the children to a secluded part of the classroom, getting on their level, making eye contact, and using a soothing tone. This increases the likelihood of the children responding favorably to the negotiation and helping to solve the conflict.

In retrospect, I wish I had discussed in advance the limits for acceptable play with the whole class. That way, when children had deviated from the acceptable play, when they hit the baby dolls or declared war on the block area, I could have referred them to that discussion to help them think through what was okay, what wasn't, and why. Keep in mind, participating in the play yourself also helps to nip inappropriate behavior in the bud.

"What's My Role?": Boosting Children's Interaction With Text

Your active participation in play, of course, offers benefits beyond stemming inappropriate behavior. It allows you to get down on the children's level and do what you do best: Teach. And in doing so, you will also boost children's interaction with text.

For example, you can show children the uses of literacy materials, encourage them to interact with texts and to produce texts themselves.

During dramatic play, teachers can model real-world uses of text, "sell" how fun interacting with text can be, and use text to welcome newcomers into an established group, with comments such as, "You could be the customer. Read this list of flavors and tell the shopkeeper what you'd like to order."

If children are perfectly happy playing ice cream parlor without ever referring to text, show them how fun using text can be. Here's what that might look like in action: If you're a customer, you say, "I'd like to order an ice cream cone, please."

The child says, "What flavor do you want?"

You respond, "I'm not sure. What flavors do you have?"

The child looks at the colors of her ice cream and says, "Chocolate, vanilla, and strawberry." You could simply order or you could say, "Hmm. It would help me if you had a sign that said that. If I go get you some paper, could you make a sign listing your flavors?" That way, you show the child the importance of environmental text and give her a solid reason to create it.

Concluding Thoughts

Thinking through your objectives for dramatic play helps you locate where it will happen, find the right materials for it, determine how you want children to carry it out, and support them in the act. This thoughtful, purposeful approach can make the difference between empty play and rich play—play that contributes to children's growth as readers, writers, and thinkers.

Chapter 7

Frequently Asked Questions About Dramatic Play

I've been traveling the country for many years, working with preschool teachers. If I've learned anything in that time, it's that those teachers have questions. Lots of questions. Here are the ones I'm asked most often, along with answers that I hope you will find helpful.

I have kids who never want to leave the dress-up area. What should I do?

You may have designed a dress-up area that is so appealing, some children never want to leave it. Good for you! It may also be that you have some children who feel safer in the dress-up area and seldom choose to go to any other part of your classroom. How do you get them to leave?

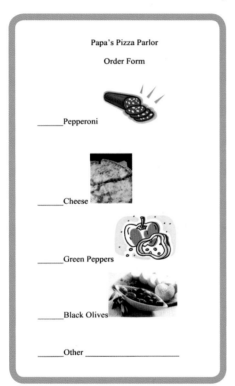

This teacher-made order form is useful to children because it contains both text and pictures. However, keep in mind, adult-child interaction around the text is key. Be sure to guide children with questions such as, "That says 'pepperoni.' Those are the pieces of meat that are circles. Did you want that on your pizza?" Also, be sure children can identify the pictures. If they can't, a form like this may not provide them with enough support.

My first answer is that you don't. If the child feels most comfortable in the dress-up area, perhaps his pretend play in that area is addressing an emotional need. This area is his "safe zone." Rather than removing the child from the area, it may be wiser to bring opportunity to him. Introduce thematic counting, sorting, and literacy activities and accompanying materials into the dress-up area. Transform it into a dramatic play area. For example, if you transformed the dress-up area into a pizza parlor, you might include different colored felt pieces cut like pepperoni, green peppers, mushrooms, etc., that the child could sort. A class-made cookbook might include a simple recipe for making a pizza that the child could follow. You could build the child's vocabulary by helping him with ordering, cooking, and serving pizza to the customers. The customers might order from menus made up of pictures and words. The server could write down orders on a form like the one pictured here. Books such as *Pete's a Pizza* by William Steig could be included in a book bin in the area. In short, make sure that the safe zone is also a literacy-rich zone. Other curriculum areas can be supported in this way as well, as long as you truly believe in the power of dramatic play.

Our program is so academic. I don't have time for dramatic play. Any advice?

As I mentioned earlier, dramatic play can support many curricular areas. You may find that some concepts don't make sense to children when you teach them in small or large groups. But when you combine that instruction with play, students make those concepts their own. For example, consider how children learn vocabulary. In many classrooms, teachers introduce vocabulary words to the whole class before they read aloud a book. When the book is read to them, they hear the words, but they remain abstract until they have a chance to use them on their own. To illustrate, years ago, I shared *Make Way for Ducklings* by Robert McCloskey with my class of four-year-olds. Not knowing any better, I read the book only once to the children. (Today we know that repeated readings help greatly in improving children's comprehension and vocabulary acquisition. See Therrien, 2004, for example.) After the reading, however, I had the children go to the dress-up area where I had created a nest from a small swimming pool and half a bale of straw. The children reenacted the story in such detail that one pretend Mama Duck announced that someone had better get her some food because she was molting and couldn't move! (Imagine how rich their understanding would have been with multiple readings!) This kind of deep understanding of the text is tough to develop.

Like any concept, you have to ask yourself: "What is the best way to teach it?" In many cases, the answer is *play*. Play provides children at all levels with opportunities for deep understanding, to make concepts their own, to build world knowledge that they can bring to future readings, and to see authentic, multiple purposes of print.

What should I do about kids who get overly aggressive?

There will always be children who are more socially skilled than others. Some children learn easily that there are certain ways to behave in a group and others don't. A wonderful resource for teaching prosocial behaviors is *Guiding Children's Social Development and Learning* (Kostelnik et al., 2008). The authors offer wonderful advice on promoting social skills, building children's friendships, and addressing aggressive behavior, while describing the language children need to negotiate their problems. The key is to let children know your expectations in advance. Children rarely "misbehave." Instead, they simply behave. The "mis" is a mismatch of expectations. So make your expectations clear from the very first day. For example, before allowing anyone to play with the materials, talk about how you'll know if anyone is treating the materials in a destructive way. Say, "I have some great new flannel board pieces out today. Many of them are wild animals. How do you think we should use them?" Invite children to answer. Toss out some tricky situations for them to consider, "What if someone uses the tiger to bite a friend?" Someone in the group will most certainly say that is not okay. "What should we do if that happens?" Listen to the suggestions and discuss the most agreeable solution. I call this pre-conflict negotiation. Discussing the potential conflict in advance helps children make smart choices later.

Once children understand what is acceptable and what isn't, they are ready to play. If a child *does* use the tiger to bite someone, move in to redirect the behavior by:

1. Labeling the behavior: *You're using the tiger to hurt someone.*

2. Indicating the effect of the behavior: *Chrissy feels angry when you hurt her.*

3. Stating the limit: *If you'd like to play with these materials, you'll have to treat them and your friends more gently.*

4. Stating the consequence: *You can either be gentle or you can select another activity.*

5. Following through: *You're showing me that you'd rather play in another area. I'll help you pick these up and move to another area.*

6. Positively reinforcing improved behavior: *You've thought of a way to use the materials gently in this area. I bet your friends are happy to play with you.*

The key to success is consistency. Over time, I suspect, you'll need only go to step 1 to stop antisocial behavior. You'll also find children themselves using these guidelines to negotiate situations.

What you may truly be asking here is, what if the kids *like* playing in rough ways? I'm sure most of us have experienced the superhero play, war play, hunting play, or reenactment of some violent story. Some children seem to have a real need for this, and teachers everywhere struggle with it. In many classrooms, teachers simply ban any play with a violent theme. I did. For 15 years I declared my classroom a "War-Toys-Free Zone."

Increasingly, though, given the violent, often scary world in which we live, some teachers are wondering if they should deal with this issue in a different way. In *Under Deadman's Skin: Discovering the Meaning of Children's Violent Play*, Jane Katch shares her conflict with watching children play out violent themes and eventually comes to terms with it by seeing it as an invitation to help children think about violence within the safety of their classrooms. Here in Maine, my colleague Mary Ellin Logue (2008) has used literacy to help children try to make sense of "Bad Guy" play. Children wrote letters to the Bad Guys asking them to leave, and the Bad Guys wrote back telling the children that they wanted to play but didn't know how to be nice. These exchanges provided opportunities for teachers to discuss Bad Guy play with children openly. While many of us may never feel completely comfortable with Bad Guy play, we may be able to find ways to live with the play, help children gain social skills, and use literacy to do it.

Dramatic play seems to require so much work. Is it really worth it?

Yes, it is worth it. And it doesn't require a lot of work, if you're creative. Here's my advice: Divide and conquer with a colleague. If each of you makes three lit kits and a dramatic play prop box, you'll be well on your way to starting a collection of materials that you can both draw on. Once you see how children respond to the kits, boxes, trunks, and other tools, you will likely want to do more.

Working with the children during play requires work, too. But it results in exciting things for them. Your interaction will stretch children's imaginations, build their vocabulary, and deepen their comprehension of the texts you read to them. You can also help them create texts. In short, you'll help them see themselves as competent literacy learners. It's worth it.

We seem to attract only girls to the dress-up area. What can I do?

Like everything about teaching, you'll get maximum results if you keep children's interests in mind. For instance, a housekeeping area may turn off some children, boys *and* girls. If that's the case, consider what you know about those children's interests. What does their play outdoors and in the block area look like? Do they play rescue games? If so, consider creating a fire-station area. If you have a child who's into a particular thing, such as sharks, trains, or dinosaurs, create a dress-up area based on those topics—underwater exploration, railroad station, fossil dig, for example. Plan it, and they will come.

I get the value of dramatic play, but it feels like we're pushing kids too hard to read and write. I don't think it's developmentally appropriate, do you?

So many of us are under pressure to push children into a curriculum that might be a better fit for older children. The reality, though, is that what I'm advocating is *play*. Play that is enriched by literacy. Play that is enriched by community. Play that is enriched by the artifacts you offer. Children are naturally interested in the world around them. Unlike things they can learn by playing independently (such as block buildings tip over when they are heavier on the top than on the bottom), literacy concepts, skills, and understandings must be taught. They have to be *learned from someone else*. Children cannot learn the names of the letters if no one ever tells

After engaging in spaceship play, two children created this picture and then told separate stories, which their teacher wrote down.

them. They won't learn sound-symbol relationships if they haven't been shown letters and the sounds that go with them. They can't learn how books work if they've never been read to. All of these are important precursors to conventional reading. In the early years, we have the luxury of playfully teaching these concepts. We support emerging skills and understandings in fun, engaging ways by allowing children to play with books, write their own stories, make their own maps and signs and, in general, by showing them the value of engaging with and creating text. When it's time for conventional reading and writing, they'll be prepared for having been in your program!

What do I say to parents who think we're "just playing"?

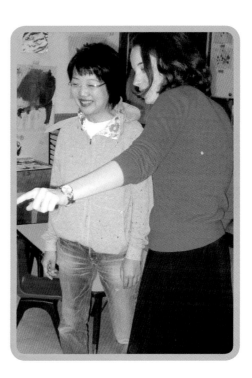

There is a large and growing body of research on the value of play that shows "just playing" isn't really a bad thing. (See for example Vukelich, 1990; Christie, 1991; Paley, 2005; Elkind, 2007.) What I suspect is that behind the parent's concern is the desire to know what the children are learning from the experience. The purpose of this book is to offer you some insights into the fact that children's social language, vocabulary, world knowledge, genre awareness, production of text, and ability to retell stories are enhanced by play experiences. Sometimes inviting the parent to come and watch the children in action while you narrate what is going on can help them understand the rich, important ways you are building their children's emerging reading and writing skills.

Concluding Thoughts

Every time a teacher asks me a question, I'm thrilled because it proves she is thinking about making dramatic play, and play in general, a big part of her children's lives. I'm always tickled when she realizes that children can play *and* learn at the same time. Not only does that realization transform the teacher, but her children as well. It's like someone waved a magic wand. I hope this book will help you tap the magic of play for yourself!

Children's Books Cited

Aardema, V. (1992). *Who's in rabbit's house?* New York: Puffin.

Ahlberg, A. (1986). *The jolly postman.* Boston: Little, Brown.

Ahlberg, J., & Alberg, A. (1991). *The jolly Christmas postman.* Boston: Little Brown.

Arlon, P. (2006). *Insect* (DK EyeKnow Books). New York: DK Publishing.

Arnosky, J. (1997). *Rabbits & raindrops.* New York: Putnam Juvenile.

Baker, A. (1999). *Brown rabbit's shape book.* London: Kingfisher.

Barton, B. (1993). *Dinosaurs, dinosaurs.* New York: HarperTrophy.

Brett, J. (2005). *Honey. . . honey. . . lion!* New York: Putnam.

Brett, J. (1990). *The mitten.* New York: Scholastic.

Brown, M. W. (1989). *The big red barn.* New York: Scholastic.

Cannon, J. (1993). *Stellaluna.* San Diego, CA: Harcourt.

Carle, E. (1994). *The very hungry caterpillar.* New York: Philomel Books.

Craig, H., & Holabird, K. (1991). *Alexander and the dragon.* London: ABC/The All Children's Company.

Crews, D. (1978). *Freight train.* New York: Greenwillow Books.

Davies, N. (2005). *Surprising sharks.* Cambridge, ME: Candlewick Press.

Delafosse, C., & Jeunesse, G. (1999). *Under the sea.* New York: Scholastic.

Dorling Kindersley (2005). *Dogs.* New York: DK Publishing.

Dorling Kindersley (2003). *Cats.* New York: DK Publishing.

Ehlert, L. (1990). *Growing vegetable soup.* New York: Voyager Books.

Ehlert, L. (1999). *Snowballs.* New York: Voyager Books.

Fleming, D. (1998). *In the small, small pond.* New York: Henry Holt and Co.

Galdone, P. (1981). *Three billy goats gruff.* New York: Clarion Books.

Guarino, D. (1989). *Is your mama a llama?* New York: Scholastic.

Hutchins, P. (1989). *The doorbell rang.* New York: HarperTrophy.

Jonas, A. (1989). *Color dance.* New York: Greenwillow Books.

Karas, G. B. (1994). *I know an old lady.* New York: Scholastic.

Keats, E. J. (1999). *Over in the meadow.* New York: Puffin.

Keats, E. J. (1962). *The snowy day.* New York: Penguin Putnam.

Lionni, L. (1963). *Swimmy.* New York: Knopf.

Marshall, J. (1997). *Goldilocks and the three bears.* New York: Penguin Putnam.

Martin, B. Jr., & Carle, E. (1967). *Brown bear, brown bear, what do you see?* New York: Holt, Rinehart, & Winston.

Martin, B. Jr. & Archambault, J. (1989). *Chicka chicka boom boom.* New York: Simon and Schuster.

McCloskey, R. (1948). *Blueberries for Sal.* New York: Viking.

McCloskey, R. (1941). *Make way for ducklings.* New York: Viking.

McKee, D. (1989). *Elmer.* New York: HarperCollins.

McMillan, B. (1996). *One, two, one pair.* New York: Scholastic.

Munsch, R. (1992). *The paper bag princess.* Toronto: Annick Press.

Murphy, S. (1996). *The best bug parade.* New York: HarperTrophy.

Murphy, S. (1996). *A pair of socks.* New York: HarperTrophy.

O'Connor, J. (2006). *Fancy Nancy.* New York: HarperCollins.

Raffi (1987). *Down by the bay.* New York: Crown.

Raffi (1993). *Everything grows.* New York: Dragonfly Books.

Rathmann, P. (1994). *Good night, gorilla.* New York: G. P. Putnam's Sons.

Shaw, C. G. (1988). *It looked like spilt milk.* New York: HarperTrophy.

Siebert, P. (2001). *The three little pigs.* Worthington, OH: Brighter Child.

Slobodkina, E. (1975). *Caps for sale.* New York: HarperCollins.

Steggall, S. (2005). *On the road.* LaHoya, CA: Kane/Miller.

Steig, W. (2000). *Pete's a pizza.* New York: Red Fox Publishing.

Steig, W. (1969). *Sylvester and the magic pebble.* New York: Trumpet.

Tomkins, J. (1981). *The catalog.* Seattle, WA: Green Tiger Press.

Tresselt, A. (1989). *The mitten.* New York: HarperTrophy.

Trivizas, E. (1997). *The three little wolves and the big bad pig.* New York: Aladdin.

Waddell, M. (2002). *Owl babies.* Cambridge, MA: Candlewick Press.

Walsh, E. S. (1991). *Mouse count.* San Diego, CA: Harcourt.

Walsh, E. S. (2000). *Mouse magic.* San Diego, CA: Harcourt.

Walsh, E. S. (1989). *Mouse paint.* San Diego, CA: Harcourt.

Wood, D. & A. (1997). *Piggies.* Orlando, FL: Voyager Books.

Professional Resources Cited

Christie, J. F. (1991). *Play and early literacy development*. New York: State University of New York.

Duke, N. K., & Bennett-Armistead, V. S. (2003). *Reading and writing informational text in the primary grades: Research-based practices*. New York: Scholastic.

Elkind, D. (2007). *The power of play: Learning what comes naturally*. New York: DaCapo Press.

Katch, J. (2002). *Under deadman's skin: Discovering the meaning of children's violent play*. Boston: Beacon Press.

Kostelnik, M., Whiren, A., Soderman, A., & Gregory, K. (2008). *Guiding children's social development and learning*. Florence, KY: Delmar Cengage Learning.

Kostelnik, M., Whiren, A., & Stein, L. (1986). Living with he-man: Managing superhero fantasy play. *Young Children, 41*(4), 3–9.

Logue, M. E., & Shelton, H. (2008). The stories bad guys tell: Promoting literacy & social awareness in preschool. *The Constructivist*. http://www.odu.edu/educ/act/journal/index.html

Morrow, L. M. (1985). Retelling stories: A strategy for improving young children's comprehension, concept of story structure, and oral language complexity. *Elementary School Journal, 85*, 647–661.

Neuman, S. B., & Roskos, K. (1993). Access to print for children of poverty: Differential effects of adult mediation and literacy-enriched play settings on environmental and functional print tasks. *American Educational Research Journal, 30*, 95–122.

Paley, V. G. (2005). *A child's work: The importance of fantasy play*. Chicago: University of Chicago Press.

Sulzby, E. (1985). Children's emergent reading of favorite storybooks: A developmental study. *Reading Research Quarterly, 20*, 458–481.

Therrien, W. (2004). Fluency and comprehension gains as a result of repeated reading: A meta-analysis. *Remedial and Special Education, 25*.

Vukelich, C. (1990). Where's the paper? Literacy during dramatic play. *Childhood Education, 66*, 205–209.

Wilmes, L. & D. (1997). *Felt board fingerplays*. Elgin, IL: Building Blocks.

Favorite Children's Books Organized by Theme

The following books are organized around popular themes used in early-childhood education. Use them to start thinking about what to include in your own collections of lit kits, prop boxes, and theme trunks. Enjoy!

Art

Baker, Alan. (1999). *White rabbit's color book*. London: Kingfisher.

Brown, Laurene K. (1992). *Visiting the art museum*. New York: Puffin.

Browne, Anthony. (2003). *The shape game*. New York: Farrar, Straus and Giroux.

Carle, Eric. (1988). *The mixed-up chameleon*. New York: HarperTrophy.

Carle, Eric. (2001). *Little cloud*. New York: Putnam Juvenile.

Day, Eileen. (2003). *I'm good at making art*. Chicago: Heinemann.

De Brunhoff, Laurent. (2003). *Babar's museum of art*. New York: Harry N. Abrams.

Editors at Phaidon Press. (2007). *The art book for children, book two*. London: Phaidon Press Inc.

Henry, Sandi. (2007). *Making amazing art: 40 activities using the 7 elements of art design*. Nashville, TN: Williamson Books.

Jonas, Ann. (1989). *Color dance*. New York: Greenwillow.

Lionni, Leo. (1995). *Little blue and little yellow*. New York: HarperTrophy.

Mayers, Florence C. (1986). *Museum of fine arts, Boston*. Boston: HNA Books.

The (NY) Metropolitan Museum of Art. (2002). *Museum ABC*. New York: Little, Brown Young Readers.

The (NY) Metropolitan Museum of Art. (2004). *Museum ABC nesting blocks*. New York: Little, Brown Young Readers.

Micklethwait, Lucy. (2004). *Animals: a first art book*. London: Frances Lincoln.

Micklethwait, Lucy. (2005). *Colors: A first art book*. London: Frances Lincoln.

Micklethwait, Lucy. (1993). *Child's book of art.* New York: DK Children.

Press, Judy. (1994). *The little hands art book: Exploring arts & crafts with 2- to 6-year-olds.* Nashville, TN: Williamson Little Hands Series.

Raczka, Bob. (2007). *Artful reading (Bob Raczka's art adventures).* Minneapolis, MN: Millbrook Press.

Reader's Clubhouse. (2007). *Mixing colors is fun (Reader's Clubhouse, level 3).* New York: Barron's Educational Series.

Shaw, Charles G. (1988). *It looked like spilt milk.* New York: HarperTrophy.

Walsh, Ellen S. (1995). *Mouse paint.* New York: Harcourt, Inc. (Red Wagon Books).

Wellington, Monica. (2000). *Squeaking of art, the mice go to the museum.* New York: Dutton Juvenile.

Babies

Ballard, Robin. (2002). *I used to be the baby.* New York: Greenwillow.

Brown, Marc. (1990). *Arthur's baby.* New York: Little Brown.

Cole, Joanna. (1997). *I'm a big brother.* New York: HarperCollins.

Cole, Joanna. (1997). *I'm a big sister.* New York: HarperCollins.

Cole, Joanna. (2000). *The new baby at your house.* New York: William Morrow and Company.

Corey, Dorothy. (1995). *Will there be a lap for me?* Morton Grove, IL: Albert Whitman & Company.

Falwell, Cathryn. (1993). *We have a baby.* New York: Clarion.

Gutman, Anne. (2003). *Lisa's baby sister (Misadventures of Gaspard and Lisa).* New York: Knopf.

Henkes, Kevin. (1990). *Julius, the baby of the world.* New York: Scholastic.

Kubler, Annie. (2000). *Waiting for baby.* Wiltshire, UK: Child's-Play.

Lasky, Kathryn. (2003). *Love that baby!* Cambridge, MA: Candlewick Press.

Mayer, Mercer. (2001). *The new baby.* New York: Random House.

Murkoff, Heidi. (2001). *What to expect when the new baby comes home.* New York: HarperFestival.

Rockwell, Lizzy. (2000). *Hello baby!* New York: Dragonfly Books.

Rosenberg, Maxine B. (1997). *Mommy's in the hospital having a baby.* New York: Clarion.

Sears, M., Sears, W., & Kelly, C. W. (2001). *Baby on the way.* New York: Little, Brown Young Readers.

Sears, M., Sears, W., & Kelly, C. W. (2001). *What baby needs.* New York: Little, Brown Young Readers.

Stein, Sara. (1995). *Oh baby!* New York: Walker & Company.

Weninger, Brigitte. (1997). *Will you mind the baby, Davy?* New York: North-South Books.

Bakery

Anderson, Catherine. (2005). *La panaderia/bread bakery.* Chicago: Heinemann.

Buchheimer, Naomi. (1956). *Let's go to the bakery.* New York: Putnam.

Carle, Eric. (1998). *Walter the baker.* New York: Aladdin.

Carle, Eric. (2005). *Pancakes, pancakes!* New York: Aladdin.

Cole, Joanna. (1995). *The magic school bus gets baked in a cake: A book about kitchen chemistry.* New York: Scholastic.

Ericson, Jennifer. (2002). *Out and about at the bakery.* Mankato, MN: Picture Window Books.

Flanagan, Alice K. (1998). *Mr. Santizo's tasty treats.* New York: Children's Press.

Greene, Carol. (1998). *Bakers make many things: Community helpers series.* Mankato, MN: Child's World Inc.

Hughes, Sarah. (2000). *My grandfather works in a bakery.* New York: Children's Press.

Jenness, Aylette. (1978). *The bakery factory: Who puts the bread on your table.* New York: HarperCollins.

Kako, Satoshi. (2007). *Mr. Crow's bakery.* Tokyo: RIC Publishing.

Mannheim, Grete. (1970). *The baker's children: A visit to a family bakery.* New York: Knopf.

Mora, Pat. (2001). *The bakery lady/la senora de la panaderia.* Houston, TX: Pinata Books.

Murphy, P. S. (2006). *The brothers' bakery.* Victoria, BC: Trafford Publishing.

Ogburn, Jacqueline K. (2005). *The bake shop ghost.* New York: Houghton Mifflin.

Pohl, Kathleen. (2006). *What happens at a bakery?* New York: Weekly Reader Early Learning Library.

Pope, Billy. (1969). *Your world: Let's visit a bakery.* Dallas, TX: Taylor Pub. Co.

Rau, Dana Meachen. (2001). *Uncle's bakery.* Mankato, MN: Compass Point Books.

Wills, J. (1991). *Amy at the bakery.* New York: Scholastic Young Hippo.

Wing, Natasha. (1996). *Jalapeno bagels.* New York: Atheneum.

Ziegler, Sandra. (1987). *A visit to the bakery.* New York: Children's Press.

Birds

Arnold, Caroline. (2003). *Birds: Nature's magnificent flying machines.* Watertown, MA: Charlesbridge Publishing.

Barlowe, Sy. (2000). *Beginning birdwatcher's book: With 48 stickers.* Mineola, NY: Dover Publications.

Boring, Mel. (1998). *Birds, nests, & eggs.* Minnetonka, MN: Northword.

Bunting, Eve. (2007). *Hurry! hurry!* San Diego, CA: Harcourt Children's Books.

Burnie, David. (2004). *Bird (DK Eyewitness Books).* New York: DK Publishing.

Denchfield, Nick. (2007). *Charlie chick.* New York: Red Wagon Books.

Fowler, Allan. (1999). *These birds can't fly.* Danbury, CT: Children's Press.

Fowler, Richard. (1996). *Little chick's big adventure.* New York: Doubleday.

Gallo, Frank. (2001). *Birds calls (Play the sounds, pull the tabs).* Norwalk, CT: Innovative Kids.

Harrison, George. (1997). *Backyard bird watching for kids: How to attract, feed, and provide homes for birds.* Minocqua, WI: Willow Creek Press.

Herkert, Barbara. (2001). *Birds in your backyard.* Nevada City, CA: Dawn Publications.

Holub, Joan. (2004). *Why do birds sing?* New York: Puffin.

Jenkins, Martin. (2003). *The emperor's egg: Read and wonder big book.* Cambridge, MA: Candlewick Press.

Kwitz, Mary Deball. (1995). *Little chick's friend duckling.* New York: HarperTrophy.

Lester, Helen. (2006). *Tacky the penguin.* New York: Houghton Mifflin/Walter Lorraine Books.

McBratney, Sam. (2000). *Just you and me.* Cambridge, MA: Candlewick Press.

McCloskey, Robert. (1941). *Make way for ducklings.* New York: Viking Kestrel Picture Books.

Rogers, Paul. (1995). *Quacky duck.* New York: Little Brown.

Root, Phyllis. (2003). *One duck stuck.* Cambridge, MA: Candlewick Press.

Schindel, John. (2000). *Busy penguins.* Berkeley, CA: Tricycle Press.

Sierra, Judy. (2003). *Antarctic antics: A book of penguin poems.* Orlando, FL: Voyager Books.

Sill, Cathryn. (1997). *About birds: A guide for children.* Atlanta, GA: Peachtree Publishers.

Sjonger, Rebecca. (2005). *Birds of all kinds (What kind of animal is it?).* New York: Crabtree Publishing.

Tafuri, Nancy. (2007). *Whose chick are you?* New York: Greenwillow.

Tankard, Jeremy. (2007). *Grumpy bird.* New York: Scholastic.

Tatham, Betty. (2001). *Penguin chick (Let's-read-and-find-out-science).* New York: HarperTrophy.

Urbanovic, Jackie. (2007). *Duck at the door.* New York: HarperCollins.

Waddell, Martin. (2002). *Owl babies.* Cambridge, MA: Candlewick Press.

Zaritzky, Bernard. (2000). *Little white duck.* New York: Little Brown.

Boats

Allen, Pamela. (1996). *Who sank the boat?* New York: Putnam Juvenile.

Barton, Byron. (1994). *Boats.* New York: HarperFestival.

Buell, Janet. (2005). *Sail away, little boat.* Brookfield, CT: Carolrhoda Books.

Bunting, Eve. (2004). *Little Bear's little boat.* New York: Bloomsbury Publishing PLC.

Collicutt, Paul. (2001). *This boat.* New York: Farrar, Straus and Giroux.

Crews, Donald. (1987). *Harbor.* New York: HarperTrophy.

Crews, Donald. (2000). *Sail away.* New York: HarperTrophy.

Demarest, Chris L. (1998). *My blue boat.* Orlando, FL: Voyager Books.

DeSeve, Randall. (2007) *Toy boat.* New York: Philomel.

Flack, Marjorie (1991). *Boats on the river.* New York: Viking Juvenile.

Guiberson, Brenda Z. (1993). *Lobster boat.* New York: Henry Holt & Co.

Hillert, Margaret. (1980). *Yellow boat.* Carlsbad, CA: Modern Curriculum Press.

Mandel, Peter. (2004). *Boats on the river.* New York: Cartwheel Books.

McDonnell, Flora. (1995). *I love boats.* Cambridge, MA: Candlewick Press.

McMenemy, Sarah. (2005). *Jack's new boat.* Cambridge, MA: Candlewick Press.

Mitton, Tony. (2005). *Busy boats.* London: Kingfisher.

Mody, Monica. (1997) *Barney's book of boats.* New York: Scholastic.

Monfried, Lucia. (1993). *Daddies boat.* New York: Puffin.

Mueller, Ross. (2007). *The boy who built the boat.* East Melbourne, VIC, Australia: Allen & Unwin.

Pallotta, Jerry. (2003). *The boat alphabet book.* Watertown, MA: Charlesbridge Publishing.

Polacco, Patricia. (1989). *Boat ride with Lillian Two Blossoms.* New York: Philomel.

Rockwell, Anne. (1993). *Boats.* New York: Puffin.

Scarry, Richard. (1997). *Busytown boat race (Busy World, Richard Scarry #6).* New York: Aladdin Paperbacks.

Tagore, Rabindranath. (1992). *Paper boats.* Honesdale, PA: Boyds Mills Press.

Trapani, Iza. (2002). *Row, row, row your boat.* Watertown, MA: Charlesbridge Publishing.

Wilkinson, Philip. (1999). *Ships.* New York: Kingfisher.

Insects and Spiders

Arlon, P. (2006). *Insect (DK EyeKnow Books).* New York: DK Publishing.

Brown, Margaret Wise. (1999). *I like bugs (Step into reading, step 1).* New York: Random House Books for Young Readers.

Chapman, Keith. (2006). *Itsy bitsy spider.* Wilton, CT: Tiger Tales.

Clarke, Ginjer L. (2007). *Bug out! The world's creepiest, crawliest critters.* New York: Grosset & Dunlap.

Drachman, Eric. (2001). *Leo the lightning bug.* Los Angeles: Kidwick Books.

Dussling, Jennifer. (2001). *DK big readers: Bugs! bugs! bugs!* New York: DK Children.

Editors at Time for Kids. (2005). *Time for kids: Spiders!* New York: HarperTrophy.

Greenaway, Theresa. (2000). *Big book of bugs.* New York: DK Children.

Kirk, David. (2006). *Ant-tuition.* New York: Grosset & Dunlap.

Kirk, David. (2006). *Miss Spider's tea party.* New York: Cartwheel Books.

Kirk, David. (2003). *Little Miss Spider.* New York: Scholastic Inc.

Kirk, David. (2003). *Little Miss Spider at Sunny Patch School.* New York: Scholastic Inc.

Lexau, Joan. (1980). *The spider makes a web.* New York: Scholastic Paperbacks.

Llewellyn, Claire. (2005). *The best book of bugs.* New York: Kingfisher.

Monks, Lydia. (2004). *Aaaarrgghh! Spider!* New York: Houghton Mifflin.

Murphy, Stuart J. (1996). *The best bug parade.* New York: HarperTrophy.

Rabe, Tish. (1999). *On beyond bugs: All about insects.* New York: Random House Books for Young Readers.

Raffi. (2002). *Spider on the floor.* New York: Alfred Knopf Books for Young Readers.

Rockwell, Anne. (2001). *Bugs are insects.* New York: HarperTrophy.

Shields, Carol Diggory. (2005). *The bugliest bug.* Cambridge, MA: Candlewick Press.

Taback, Simms. (1997). *There was an old lady who swallowed a fly.* New York: Viking Juvenile.

Castles

Amery, Heather. (1996). *Castle tales.* London: Usborne Books.

Brochard, Philippe. (1982). *Castles of the middle ages.* Needham, MA: Silver Burdett Pr.

Buehr, Walter. (1957). *Knights, castles and feudal life.* New York: G. P. Putnam's Sons.

Daynes, Katie. (2005). *See inside castles.* London: Usborne Publishing Ltd.

DK Publishing. (2005). *Castle and knight.* New York: DK Children.

Farre, Marie R. (1988). *Long ago in a castle: What was it like living safe behind castle walls?* Ossining, NY: Young Discovery Library.

Gal, Laszlo. (1995). *Merlin's castle.* Markham, ON: Fitzhenry and Whiteside.

Geis, Alissa Imre. (2004). *Neil's castle.* New York: Viking Juvenile.

Golden Books. (1994). *The knight's castle: A pop-up book.* New York: Golden Books.

Graves, Robert. (1991). *An ancient castle.* New York: M. Kesend Publishing.

Grimes, Lee. (1990). *Fortune cookie castle.* New York: Dutton Juvenile.

Ichikawa, Satomi. (1986). *Nora's castle.* New York: Philomel.

Jeunesse, Gallimard. (1993). *Castles.* New York: Scholastic.

Kates, Molly. (1996). *The little castle.* New York: Random House Books for Young Readers.

Munsch, Robert. (2005). *The sandcastle contest.* New York: Cartwheel Books.

Nicoll, Helen. (1985). *Meg's castle.* New York: Puffin.

Osband, Gillian. (1993). *Castles.* London: Tango Books.

Smythe, M. (1985). *Build your own castle.* London: Franklin Watts.

Yee, Brenda. (1999). *Sand castle.* New York: Greenwillow.

Dinosaurs

Aliki. (1990). *Dinosaur bones.* New York: HarperTrophy.

Aliki. (1988). *Digging up dinosaurs.* New York: HarperCollins.

Barton, Byron. (1990). *Bones, bones, dinosaur bones.* New York: HarperCollins.

Boynton, Sandra. (1993). *Oh my oh my oh dinosaurs!* New York: Workman.

Cole, Joanna. (1995). *The magic school bus in the time of the dinosaurs.* New York: Scholastic.

DK Publishing. (1994). *Big book of dinosaurs.* New York: DK Children.

Most, Bernard. (1984). *If the dinosaurs came back.* Orlando, FL: Voyager Books.

Most, Bernard. (1984). *Whatever happened to the dinosaurs?* New York: Harcourt Children's Books.

Most, Bernard. (1993). *The littlest dinosaurs.* Pine Plains, NY: Live Oak Media.

Most, Bernard. (1995). *How big were the dinosaurs?* Orlando, FL: Voyager Books.

Pallotta, Jerry. (1990). *The dinosaur alphabet book.* Watertown, MA: Charlesbridge Publishing.

Priddy, Roger. (2004). *My big dinosaur book.* London: Priddy Books.

Rey, Margret. (1989). *Curious George and the dinosaur.* New York: Houghton Mifflin.

Schnetzler, Pattie. (1996). *Ten little dinosaurs picture book.* Denver, CO: Accord.

Scholastic. (2007). *My first jumbo book of dinosaurs.* New York: Scholastic.

Stickland, Paul. (2000). *Ten terrible dinosaurs.* New York: Puffin.

Stickland, Paul. (1996). *Dinosaur stomp.* New York: Dutton Juvenile.

Stickland, Paul and Strickland, Henrietta. (2002). *Dinosaur roar!* New York: Puffin.

Yolen, Jane. (2004). *How do dinosaurs clean their rooms?* New York: Blue Sky Press.

Zimmerman, Howard. (2000). *Dinosaurs: The biggest baddest strangest fastest.* New York: Atheneum.

Farm

Adams, Pam. (2007). *Old Macdonald had a farm.* Auburn, ME: Child's Play International.

Amery, Heather. (2006). *On the farm.* London: Usborne Books.

Black, Sonia. (2003). *On the farm.* New York: Cartwheel Books.

Boten, Wallace. (2003). *From farm to store.* Mankato, MN: Compass Point Books.

Capucilli, Alyssa Satin. (2002). *Biscuit visits the farm.* New York: HarperFestival.

Cousins, Lucy. (2001). *Maisy's morning on the farm.* Cambridge, MA: Candlewick Press.

Cowley, Joy. (2006). *Mrs. Wishy-Washy's farm.* New York: Puffin.

Cowley, Joy. (2000). *The rusty, trusty tractor.* Honesdale, PA: Boyds Mills Press.

DK Publishing (2007). *All around the farm.* New York: DK Children.

Fowler, Allan. (2000). *Living on farms*. New York: Children's Press.

Fowler, Allan. (1993). *If it weren't for farmers*. New York: Children's Press.

James, Diane. (1997). *On the farm*. Minnetoka, MN: Two-Can Publishing, Inc.

Kutner, Merrily. (2005). *Down on the farm*. New York: Holiday House.

Miller, Jane. (1987). *The farm alphabet book*. New York: Scholastic Paperbacks.

Mitton, Tony. (2005). *Tremendous tractors*. London: Kingfisher.

Nolen, Jerdine. (1998). *Harvey Potter's balloon farm*. New York: HarperTrophy.

Provensen, Alice & Martin. (1988). *Year at Maple Hill Farm*. New York: Aladdin.

Read, Helen S. (1928). *Grandfather's farm*. Farmington Hills, MI: Charles Scribner's Sons.

Shepherd, Jodie. (2006). *Farm friends*. Bath, UK: Reader's Digest.

Firefighters

Auerbach, Annie. (2003). *Three-alarm fire!* New York: Little Simon.

Bryant, Megan E. (2003). *The little engine that could and the fire rescue*. New York: Grosset & Dunlap.

Cuyler, Margery. (2004). *Stop drop and roll*. Pine Plains, NY: Live Oak Media.

Demarest, Chris L. (2003). *Firefighters A to Z*. New York: Aladdin.

Demarest, Chris L. (2002). *Here come our firefighters!* New York: Little Simon.

DK Publishing. (2003). *Fire truck*. New York: DK Children.

DK Publishing. (2002). *Touch and feel: Fire engine*. New York: DK Publishing.

Gibbons, Gail. (1987). *Fire! Fire!* New York: HarperTrophy.

Klavins, Uldis, Teitelbaum, Michael, and Walker, Jeff. (2001). *Tonka: If I could drive a fire truck!* New York: Cartwheel Books.

Kottke, Jan. (2000). *A day with firefighters*. Danbury, CT: Children's Press.

Lewison, Wendy Cheyette. (1998). *A trip to the firehouse*. New York: Grosset & Dunlap.

Liebman, Dan. (1999). *I want to be a firefighter*. Richmond Hill, ON: Firefly Books.

MacLean, Christine Kole. (2004). *Even firefighters hug their moms*. New York: Puffin.

McGuire, Leslie. (1996). *Big Frank's fire truck*. New York: Random House.

Mitton, Tony. (2000). *Flashing fire engines*. London: Kingfisher.

Parker, Marjorie Blain. (2004). *Hello, fire truck!* New York: Cartwheel Books.

Slater, Teddy. (1991). *All aboard fire trucks*. New York: Grosset & Dunlap.

Ulz, Ivan. (2005). *Fire truck!* New York: Scholastic.

Yee, Wong Herbert. (1998). *Fireman Small to the rescue*. New York: Houghton Mifflin.

Yee, Wong Herbert. (1994). *Fireman Small*. New York: Houghton Mifflin.

Flowers

Bunting, Eve. (2000). *Flower garden*. Orlando, FL: Voyager Books.

Bunting, Eve. (1999). *Sunflower house*. Orlando, FL: Voyager Books.

Burrowes, Adjoa J. (2000). *Grandma's purple flowers*. New York: Lee & Low Books.

Cole, Henry. (1997). *Jack's garden*. New York: HarperTrophy.

Cooney, Barbara. (1985). *Miss Rumphius*. New York: Puffin.

Howell, Laura. (2005). *The Usborne little book of flowers*. London: Usborne Publishing Ltd.

Jordan, Helen J. (2000). *How a seed grows*. New York: HarperTrophy.

Kemp, Anthea. (1988). *Mr. Percy's magic greenhouse*. London: Victor Gollancz.

Kemper, Bitsy. (2006). *Out and about at the greenhouse*. Mankato, MN: Picture Window Books.

Knudsen, Natalie. (2001). *Child's garden of flowers*. Ames, IA: Reiman Gardens Cohorts.

Kudlinski, Kathleen V. (1999). *Dandelions*. Minneapolis, MN: Lerner Publishing Group.

Lobel, Anita. (1996). *Alison's zinnia*. New York: HarperTrophy.

Lobel, Arnold. (1993). *The rose in my garden*. New York: HarperTrophy.

Lorenz Editors. (2002). *Let's look at flowers*. London: Lorenz Books.

Noda, Takayo. (2006). *Song of the flowers*. New York: Dial.

Pallotta, Jerry. (1989). *The flower alphabet book*. Watertown, MA: Charlesbridge Publishing.

Schaefer, Lola M. (2003). *Pick, pull, snap! Where once a flower bloomed*. New York: Greenwillow.

Schaefer, Lola M. (2000). *This is the sunflower*. New York: Greenwillow.

Stoker, Joann. (1999). *ABC book of flowers for young gardeners*. Columbia, SC: Summerhouse Press.

Trimble, Marcia. (2002). *Flower green: A flower for all seasons*. Los Altos Hills, CA: Images Press.

Wellington, Monica. (2007). *Zinnia's flower garden*. New York: Puffin.

Grocery Store

Baggette, Susan K. (1998). *Jonathan goes to the grocery store*. Sterling, VA: Brookfield Reader.

Bailey, Cindy A. (2002). *Going to the grocery store*. New York: DRL Books Inc.

Berg, Brook. (2003). *What happened to Marion's book?* Fort Atkinson, WI: Upstart Books.

Bryant, Donna. (1989). *One day at the supermarket*. Nashville, TN: Ideals Publications.

Camp, Lindsay. (1993). *Dinosaurs at the supermarket*. New York: Viking Juvenile.

Disalvo-Ryan, Dyanne. (2000). *Grandpa's corner store*. New York: HarperCollins.

Doyle, Charlotte. (2004). *Supermarket!* Cambridge, MA: Candlewick Press.

Elya, Susan Middleton. (2006). *Bebe goes shopping.* New York: Harcourt Children's Books.

Gallacher, Lorraine. (2001). *Let's go to the supermarket.* New York: Simon Spotlight/Nickelodeon.

Gordon, Margaret. (1984). *Supermarket mice.* New York: Dutton Juvenile.

Grossman, Bill. (1991). *Tommy at the grocery store.* New York: HarperTrophy.

Hill, Mary. (2003). *Signs at the store.* New York: Children's Press.

Hoena, B. A. (2004). *A visit to the supermarket.* Mankato, MN: Pebble Plus.

Klein, Adria F. (2007). *Max goes to the grocery store.* Mankato, MN: Picture Window Books.

Krull, Kathleen. (2001). *Supermarket.* New York: Holiday House.

Leblanc, Anne. (1997). *Shopping with Benjamin.* New York: Sterling Pub Co Inc.

Leeper, Angela. (2004). *Grocery store.* Chicago: Heinemann.

Meddaugh, Susan. (1994). *The witches' supermarket.* New York: Houghton Mifflin/Walter Lorraine Books.

Pan, Hui-Mei. (2004). *What's in Grandma's grocery bag?* Long Island City, NY: Star Bright Books.

Richmond, Christine. (2007). *Lost in the supermarket.* Victoria, BC: Trafford Publishing.

Schaefer, Lola. (2000). *Supermarket (Who works here?).* Chicago: Heinemann.

Library

Deedy, Carmen Agra. (1994). *The library dragon.* Atlanta, GA: Peachtree Publishers.

Fraser, Mary Ann. (2005). *I. Q. goes to the library.* New York: Walker Books for Young Readers.

Gibbons, Gail. (1988). *The book about libraries.* Orlando, FL: Voyager Books.

Gorman, Jacqueline Laks. (2005). *The library/La biblioteca.* New York: Weekly Reader Early Learning Library.

Hoena, B. A. (2003). *A visit to the library.* Mankato, MN: Pebble Plus.

Hopkins, Jackie. (2004). *The shelf elf.* Fort Atkinson, WI: Upstart Books.

Johnston, Marianne. (1999). *Let's visit the library.* New York: Powerkids Press.

Kimmel, Eric. (1992). *I took my frog to the library.* Pine Plains, NY: Live Oak Media.

McQuinn, Anna. (2006). *Lola at the library.* Watertown, MA: Charlesbridge Publishing.

Meister, Cari. (2000). *Tiny goes to the library.* New York: Puffin.

Mora, Pat. (2000). *Tomas and the library lady.* New York: Dragonfly Books.

Morris, Carla. (2007). *The boy who was raised by librarians.* Atlanta, GA: Peachtree Publishers.

Rey, H. A. (2003). *Curious George visits the library.* New York: Houghton Mifflin.

Sesame Street. (1986). *A visit to the sesame street library.* New York: Random House.

Stadler, Alexander. (2006). *Beverly Billingsly borrows a book.* Orlando, FL: Voyager Books.

Terry, Sonja. (2006). *"L" is for library.* Fort Atkinson, WI: Upstart Books.

Tester, Sylvia Root. (1986). *A visit to the library.* Danbury, CT: Children's Press.

Thompson, Carol L. (2003). *Mr. Wiggle's library.* Grand Rapids, MI: School Specialty Publishing.

Music

Auzary-Luton, Sylvie. (1999). *1 2 3 music.* New York: Scholastic.

Crozon, Alain. (2004). *What am I? Music!* Paris: Seuil.

Faine, Edward A., & Celich, Kristina L. (2003). *Bebop babies.* Takoma Park, MD: IM Press.

Gillard, Denise. (2001). *Music from the sky.* Toronto, ON: Groundwood Books.

Greenfield, Eloise. (1991). *I make music.* London: Writers & Readers Publishing.

Hayes, Phyllis. (1981). *Musical instruments you can make.* London: Franklin Watts.

Koscielniak, Bruce. (2000). *The story of the incredible orchestra: An introduction to musical instruments and the symphony orchestra.* New York: Houghton Mifflin.

Lillegard, Dee. (1988). *Strings.* New York: Children's Press.

Lillegard, Dee. (1987). *Percussion: An introduction to musical instruments.* New York: Children's Press.

McPhail, David. (2001). *Mole music.* New York: Henry Holt and Co.

Moss, Lloyd. (2003). *Music is.* New York: Putnam Juvenile.

Moss, Lloyd. (1995). *Zin! Zin! Zin! A violin.* New York: Simon & Schuster Children's Publishing.

Pinkney, Andrea Davis. (1997). *Shake shake shake.* New York: Red Wagon Books.

Shahan, Sherry. (2002). *The jazzy alphabet.* New York: Philomel.

Swados, E. (1990). *Inside out: A musical adventure.* New York: Little Brown and Company.

Tibo, Gilles. (1997). *Simon makes music.* Toronto: Tundra Books.

Ocean

Blevins, Wiley. (2006). *Ocean life.* New York: Cartwheel Books.

Burns, Kate. (1996). *Hide and seek: In the ocean.* New York: Megan Tingley.

Deprisco, Dorothea. (2003). *Who's in the ocean?* Atlanta, GA: Piggy Toes Press / Intervisual Books.

Dorros, Arthur. (2000). *Follow the water from brook to ocean.* New York: HarperTrophy.

Editors at Usborne Publishing. (2005). *Little encyclopedia of seas and oceans.* London: Usborne Publishing Ltd.

Fowler, Allan. (1996). *The earth is mostly ocean.* New York: Children's Press.

Fredericks, Anthony D. (1998). *Exploring the oceans: Science activities for kids.* Golden, CO: Fulcrum Publishing.

Hirschi, Ron. (2007). *Ocean seasons.* Mt. Pleasant, SC: Sylvan Dell Publishing.

Holmes, Steve. (2005). *Let's dive in the ocean! ¡Vamos a bucear!* Minnetonka, MN: Two-Can Publishing, Inc.

Karwoski, Gail Langer. (2007). *Water beds: Sleeping in the ocean.* Mt. Pleasant, SC: Sylvan Dell Publishing.

Lewis, Anthony. (2007). *Little ocean explorers.* Auburn, ME: Child's Play International.

Marshak, Suzanna. (1991). *I am the ocean.* New York: Arcade Publishing.

Moore, Jo Ellen. (2005). *All about the ocean.* Monterey, CA: Evan-Moor Educational Publishers.

Pallotta, Jerry. (1991). *The underwater alphabet book.* Watertown, MA: Charlesbridge Publishing.

Pallotta, Jerry. (1989). *The ocean alphabet book.* Watertown, MA: Charlesbridge Publishing.

Pledger, Maurice. (2001). *In the ocean.* San Diego, CA: Silver Dolphin Books.

Rey, H. A. (1999). *Curious George goes to the beach.* New York: Houghton Mifflin.

Ryan, Pam Muñoz. (2001). *Hello ocean.* Watertown, MA: Charlesbridge Publishing.

Stierle, Cynthia. (2007). *Ocean life from A to Z.* Bath, UK: Reader's Digest.

Thompson, D. R. (2004). *The big ocean: An underwater naptime adventure.* Tigard, OR: This New World Publishing, LLC.

Pets and Veterinarians

Ardalan, Hayde. (2001). *Milton goes to the vet.* San Francisco, CA: Chronicle Books.

Cimarusti, Marie Torres. (2004). *Peek-a-pet.* New York: Dutton Juvenile.

Dodd, Lynley. (2003). *Hairy Maclary's rumpus at the vet.* Berkeley, CA: Tricycle Press.

Donner, Andrea. (2006). *What pets teach us: Life's lesson learned from our little friends.* Minocqua, WI: Willow Creek Press.

Dr. Seuss. (2005). *Wet pet, dry pet, your pet, my pet.* New York: Random House.

Foley, Cate. (2000). *My turtle.* Danbury, CT: Children's Press.

Levine, Ellen. (1988). *If you were an animal doctor.* New York: Scholastic.

Liebman, Dan. (2000). *I want to be a vet.* Richmond Hill, ON: Firefly Books.

Lumley, Kathryn Wentzel. (1985). *I can be an animal doctor.* Danbury, CT: Children's Press.

McPhail, David. (1993). *Emma's pet.* New York: Puffin.

Miller, Margaret. (2003). *Baby pets.* New York: Little Simon.

Patrick, Jean L. S. (2003). *Cows, cats, and kids: A veterinarian's family at work.* Honesdale, PA: Boyds Mills Press.

Rey, H. A. (1998). *Curious George and the puppies.* New York: Houghton Mifflin.

Shea, Kitty. (2004). *Out and about at the vet clinic.* Mankato, MN: Picture Window Books.

Verdick, Elizabeth. (2005). *Tails are not for pulling.* Minneapolis, MN: Free Spirit Publishing.

Walker, Pam. (2000). *My goldfish.* Danbury, CT: Children's Press.

Wood, Jane R., & Haverfield, Mary. (2004). *Mocha, the real doctor.* Albany, TX: Bright Sky Press.

Pirates

Adkins, Jan. (2006). *What if you met a pirate?* New York: Roaring Brook Press.

Allen, Pamela. (1993). *I wish I had a pirate suit.* New York: Puffin.

Anastasio, Dina. (1997). *Pirates.* New York: Grosset & Dunlap.

Harris, Peter. (2006). *Night pirates.* New York: Scholastic.

Howard, Barnaby. (2006). *The best book of pirates.* London: Kingfisher.

Kennedy, Kim. (2002). *Pirate Pete.* New York: Harry N. Abrams.

Kennedy, Kim. (2006). *Pirate Pete's giant adventure.* New York: Harry N. Abrams.

Lichtenheld, Tom. (2003). *Everything I know about pirates.* New York: Aladdin.

Long, Melinda. (2003). *How I became a pirate.* New York: Harcourt.

McConnell, Sarah. (2006). *Don't mention pirates.* Hauppauge, NY: Barron's Educational Series.

McPhail, David. (1997). *Edward and the pirates.* New York: Little, Brown Young Readers.

Robins, Deri and Buchanan, George. (1995). *The great pirate activity book.* London: Kingfisher.

Schimel, Lawrence. (2007). *Little pirate goes to school.* Norwalk, CT: Innovative Kids.

Schimel, Lawrence. (2007). *Little pirate goes to bed.* Norwalk, CT: Innovative Kids.

Seaworthy, Oscar. (2007). *Port side pirates.* Cambridge, MA: Barefoot Books.

Sobel, June. (2006). *Shiver me letters: A pirate ABC.* New York: Harcourt.

Tucker, Kathy. (1997). *Do pirates take baths?* Morton Grove, IL: Albert Whitman & Company.

Watt, Fiona. (2007). *That's not my pirate.* London: Usborne Publishing Ltd.

Wigington, Patti. (2006). *Pirate's alphabet.* Warwick, NY: Moo Press.

Pizza

Auch, Mary Jane. (2003). *The princess and the pizza.* New York: Holiday House.

Barbour, Karen. (1999). *Little Nino's pizzeria.* Orlando, FL: Voyager Books.

Boniface, William. (2000). *What do you want on your pizza?* New York: Price Stern Sloan.

Buehner, Caralyn & Mark. (2004). *A job for Wittilda.* New York: Puffin.

Castaldo, Nancy F. (2005). *Pizza for the queen.* New York: Holiday House.

Dobson, Christina. (2003). *Pizza counting.* Watertown, MA: Charlesbridge Publishing.

Eberts, Marjorie. (1984). *Pancakes, crackers, and pizza: A book of shapes.* Danbury, CT: Children's Press.

Hao, K. T. (2003). *One pizza, one penny.* Peru, IL: Cricket Books.

Hill, Mary. (2002). *Let's make pizza.* Danbury, CT: Children's Press.

Holub, Joan. (2001). *The pizza that we made.* New York: Puffin.

Labatt, Mary. (2003). *Pizza for Sam.* Toronto, ON: Kids Can Press, Ltd.

Lansky, Bruce. (2006). *Peter Peter pizza eater.* Minnetonka, MN: Meadowbrook.

Pienkowski, Jan. (2002). *Pizza!* Cambridge, MA: Candlewick Press.

Rey, Margret. (1985). *Curious George and the pizza.* New York: Houghton Mifflin.

Rotner, Shelley. (1996). *Hold the anchovies!: A book about pizza.* London: Orchard Books.

Sanzari, Sylvester. (1995). *The king of pizza.* New York: Workman Publishing Company.

Schimel, Lawrence. (2004). *Fiesta con pizza/Pizza party.* Miami, FL: Panamericana.

Steig, William. (1998). *Pete's a pizza.* New York: Joanna Cotler.

Sturges, Philemon. (2002). *The little red hen (makes a pizza).* New York: Puffin.

Voake, Charlotte. (2003). *Pizza kittens.* London: Walker Books Ltd.

Walter, Virginia. (1998). *Hi, pizza man!* London: Orchard Books.

Wellington, Monica. (2006). *Pizza at Sally's.* New York: Dutton Juvenile.

Pond

Alderson, Sue Ann. (1998). *Pond seasons.* Toronto, ON: Groundwood Books.

Allman, Barbara. (2005). *All about the pond.* Monterey, CA: Evan-Moor Educational Publishers.

Curran, Eileen. (1985). *Life in the pond.* New York: Troll Communications.

Editors at Houghton Mifflin. (2004). *Animal babies in ponds and rivers.* Boston, MA: Houghton Mifflin.

Falwell, Cathryn. (2001). *Turtle splash! Countdown at the pond.* New York: Greenwillow.

Fleming, Denise. (2007). *In the small, small pond.* New York: Henry Holt and Co.

Galko, Francine. (2002). *Pond animals.* Chicago: Heinemann.

George, Lindsay Barrett. (2000). *Beaver at Long Pond.* New York: HarperTrophy.

George, William T. (1991). *Fishing at Long Pond.* New York: Greenwillow.

George, William T. (1989). *Box turtles at Long Pond.* New York: Greenwillow.

Hunter, Anne. (1999). *What's in the pond?* New York: Houghton Mifflin.

Jennings, Terry J. (1989). *Pond life.* New York: Children's Press.

Long, Lorraine. (1998). *Down at the pond.* Woodstock, GA: Periwinkle Park Educational Productions.

Mara, Wil. (2007). *The frog in the pond.* New York: Children's Press.

McDowell, Josh. (1988). *Katie's adventure at Blueberry Pond.* Elgin, IL: Chariot Family Pub.

Murphy, Robert. (1964). *The pond.* New York: Dutton.

Reid, Georte K. (1967). *Pond life.* New York: Golden Books.

Rockwell, Jane. (1984). *All about ponds.* New York: Troll Communications.

Sabin, Francene. (1982). *Wonders of the pond.* New York: Troll Communications.

Silver, Donald. (1997). *Pond.* New York: McGraw-Hill.

Restaurant

Calmenson, Stephanie. (1995). *Dinner at the Panda Palace.* New York: HarperTrophy.

Canizares, Susan. (2000). *Restaurant.* New York: Scholastic.

Hughes, Sarah. (2000). *My uncle owns a deli.* Danbury, CT: Children's Press.

London, Jonathan. (2003). *Froggy eats out.* New York: Puffin.

Loomis, Christine. (1994). *In the diner.* New York: Scholastic.

Minden, Cecilia. (2006). *Restaurant owners.* Mankato, MN: Child's World.

Miyazawa, Kenji. (2007). *The restaurant of many orders.* Tokyo: RIC Publications.

Moss, Marissa. (1999). *Mel's diner.* New York: Troll Communications.

O'Connor, Jane. (2005). *Fancy Nancy.* New York: HarperCollins.

Oxenbury, Helen. (1994). *Eating out.* New York: Puffin.

Radabaugh, Melinda Beth. (2003). *Going to a restaurant.* Chicago: Heinemann.

Rey, Margret. (1988). *Curious George goes to a restaurant.* New York: Houghton Mifflin.

Schaefer, Lola. (2001). *Fast food restaurant.* Chicago: Heinemann.

Schwarz, Michelle. (2004). *The best restaurant in the world.* New York: Dutton Juvenile.

Seidler, Ann. (1993). *The hungry thing goes to a restaurant.* New York: Scholastic.

Stevens, Janet. (2005). *Cook-a-doodle-doo.* Orlando, FL: Voyager Books.

Weeks, Sarah. (2007). *Two eggs, please.* New York: Aladdin.